Early American
Furniture-Making
Handbook

Early American Furniture-Making Handbook

BY THE STAFF OF

THE FAMILY HANDYMAN

MAGAZINE

CHARLES SCRIBNER'S SONS / NEW YORK

3 5 7 9 11 13 15 17 19 M/C 20 18 16 14 12 10 8 6 4
1 3 5 7 9 11 13 15 17 19 M/P 20 18 16 14 12 10 8 6 4 2

PRINTED IN THE UNITED STATES OF AMERICA
Library of Congress Catalog Card Number 72–38945

ISBN 0-684-12869-1 (Trade, cloth)
ISBN 0-684-15060-3 (SL, paper)

Contents

SECTION III. EARLY AMERICAN FURNITURE FINISHING

Early American
Furniture-Making
Handbook

CONSTRUCTION TECHNIQUES

for

EARLY AMERICAN

FURNITURE

What the cabinetmaker of early America lacked in artistry, he amply made up in sturdy construction. In fact, construction of this type was found so faultless that it is employed in American furniture built today.

In this section of the book, we will cover the basics of furniture construction, with special emphasis on the techniques needed to complete the projects in Section II.

WOODS YOU CAN USE

When making your own early American furniture, you have a wide selection of materials to use. In addition to fir plywood and the hardwood-veneered plywoods, you have panel materials such as smooth-surfaced hardboard, textured hardboard, plastic laminates, hardboard and other panel materials.

The two main classifications of lumber are hardwood and softwood. Hardwoods are the deciduous trees like oak, maple, and hickory, which lose their leaves in the fall. The softwoods are the evergreens or conifers like pine and spruce. These terms are slightly misleading, since you will run across hardwoods that are relatively soft and softwoods that are hard.

Hardwoods are more difficult to work with but are more durable than softwoods. They also have more attractive grains and take finishes better. They should be used where appearance and sturdiness are important factors. The common hardwoods used in early American furniture making are walnut, cherry, oak, birch and maple, in descending order of working ease, maple being the most difficult to work. The softwoods most frequently used are pine, cedar, fir and hemlock.

GRADES AND SIZES OF LUMBER

Lumber is sold according to grade and size. For commercial purposes it is standardized under two codes, one for softwoods, the other for hardwoods.

SOFTWOOD GRADES. Yard lumber is classified as Select and Common. Each of these, in turn, is graded according to quality—that is, freedom from knots, blemishes, or defects.

Select lumber is generally clear or contains only minor defects which can be covered by paint or other finishes. It is graded A, B, C, and D. Generally speaking, C Select will prove the best buy for you in Select lumber.

Common lumber contains numerous defects and blemishes which prevent its use for finishing purposes, but it is suitable for general utility or construction. It is graded as Nos. 1, 2, 3, 4, and 5. The best buy, No. 2 Common, will keep your waste at a minimum.

HARDWOOD GRADES. Hardwood grades are based on the percentage of clear cuttings that can be obtained from a piece of lumber. The system is much more difficult to understand than that of softwood. Numbered gradings are not comparable between different woods. For example, the fourth grade of mahogany is a much better wood than the fourth grade of hickory. The essential grading information is given in the chart on page 14: however, this is not complete or absolutely accurate, but it can be taken as a general guide for the purchase of hardwoods.

To save money, always buy the lowest grade of lumber that will fill your needs. If, for example, you are buying one-by-two strips for furring, shelf cleats, or garden stakes, it is foolish to buy B and Better lumber.

SIZES OF LUMBER. Manufactured lumber as shipped from the mill to the lumberyard is classified as (1) rough, (2) surfaced, and (3) worked. Rough lumber is furry and splintery. It

HARDWOOD GRADES
GENERAL GRADING—INDICATES DECREASE IN QUALITY

HARDWOODS	1ST AND 2ND GRADES	3D GRADE	4TH GRADE	5TH GRADE	6TH GRADE
Ash, beech, birch, maple, oak	Firsts and seconds	Selects	No. 1 Common	No. 2 Common	Sound Wormy
Cherry	Firsts and seconds	Selects	No. 1 Common	No. 2 Common	No. 3A Common
Chestnut	Firsts and seconds	Selects	No. 1 Common	Sound Wormy	No. 2 Common
Elm, hickory	Firsts and seconds	No. 1 Common	No. 2 Common	No. 3A Common	No. 3B Common
Walnut	Firsts and seconds	Selects	No. 1 Common	No. 2 Common	No. 3 Common
Poplar	Firsts and seconds	Sap Marks	Selects	Stained & Sap Marks	No. 1 Common

FIRSTS: 91⅔ per cent clear both sides
SECONDS: 83⅓ per cent clear both sides
FIRSTS AND SECONDS: Not less than 20 per cent firsts (best commercial grade)
SELECTS: 90 per cent clear one side

No. 1 COMMON: 66⅔ per cent clear face
No. 2 COMMON: 50 per cent clear face
No. 3A COMMON: 33⅓ per cent clear face
No. 3B COMMON: 25 per cent clear face
SOUND WORMY: No. 1 Common with wormholes

NOMINAL AND ACTUAL SIZES OF LUMBER
(INCHES)

NOMINAL THICKNESS	SOFTWOOD AVERAGE/ACTUAL THICKNESS	HARDWOOD	NOMINAL WIDTH	SOFTWOOD AVERAGE/ACTUAL WIDTH	HARDWOOD
½	$\frac{7}{16}$	½	1	$\frac{25}{32}$	⅞
1	$\frac{25}{32}$	⅞	2	1 ⅝	Usually sold to
1¼	1 ⅛	1⅛	3	2 ⅝	nearest nomi-
1½	1 $\frac{5}{16}$	1⅜	4	3 ⅝	nal size at ran-
1¾	1 ½	1⅝	6	5 ⅝	dom widths
2	1 ⅝	1¾	8	7 ½	with edges left
3	2 ⅝	2¾	10	9 ½	rough
			12	11 ½	

is generally sold to factories or large woodworking shops that can dress their own lumber. Surfaced lumber is dressed by running it through a planer machine which leaves the wood smooth. It may be surfaced on one side (S1S), two sides (S2S), one edge (S1E), two edges (S2E), or a combination of sides and edges (S1S1E or SIS2E). The number you will normally use will be dressed four sides (S4S). Worked lumber is cut into moldings. Many kinds, shapes, and sizes are stocked by the average lumberyard.

Lumber comes from the saw in nominal sizes such as two-by-four, one-by-six, and so forth. In this form it is classified as "rough" or nominal size. When run through the planer, the surface dwindles in size by the amount of wood removed. A nominal two-by-four surfaced on four sides (S4S) thus shrinks to 1⅝ by 3⅝ inches in cross section, a one-by-six board to ²⁵⁄₃₂ by 5⅝ inches (actual size). A "five-quarter" board, nominally 1¼ inches thick, actually comes to 1⅛ inches when dressed. Refer to the chart below for nominal and average actual sizes of stock lumber. In some areas of the country, the actual sizes may be slightly larger.

MOISTURE AND SHRINKAGE. Freshly cut lumber contains a good deal of moisture. As the moisture disappears, the board shrinks somewhat. When the moisture content of a board drops to about 20 per cent, the lumber is considered seasoned. For furniture and cabinet use, only stock with 6 to 12 per cent moisture content should be used. This seasoning is generally speeded by placing the wood in an oven, a process called kiln drying. Lumber with a high moisture content is difficult to work with, and when the project is finished and the lumber begins to dry out, it will shrink and may open up glued joints and seams and may even crack. For this reason, store lumber in a warm, dry place. Do not let the lumber sag, or it will warp and twist out of shape.

If you want to test wood for moisture content and shrinkage, saw off a piece 1 inch long and exactly 6 inches across the grain. Weigh it carefully. Bake in the oven at 212 degrees Fahrenheit for at least 4 hours. Then measure it or compare it to an undried piece of the same stock. To determine the moisture content, find the difference between the wet and dry weight, and divide the difference by the dry weight. *Example:* A piece weighing 16 ounces originally weighs 12 ounces after drying (difference 4 ounces), dividing 4 by 12 gives ⅓, or a moisture content of 33⅓ per cent.

LUMBER DEFECTS. Several defects must be avoided in the selection of lumber:

1. Knots are places at which the branch of a tree has caused a fibrous, woody mass to form. Sometimes, when knots are solid, this wood is in demand for such things as knotty-pine paneling, but most often knots are a defect that must be removed from furniture lumber.

2. A split is a large break in a board.

3. Check is a slight separation lengthwise in a board. This is often found at the end of the board and must be trimmed off before cutting stock to length.

4. Warp is a curve across the grain which occurs during the drying process.

5. Wind is a longitudinal twist in a board.

6. Decay is rotted area in the wood which causes a soft spot.

7. A shake is a separation of wood along the annual ring.

8. Insect damage causes small holes in the wood surface.

9. Molds and stains cause discoloration of the wood surface.

PLYWOOD. "Plywood" and "home-craftsman projects" have become almost synonymous. It is important, therefore, for you to know something of the qualities and potentialities of this relatively new material.

Plywood is much stronger than wood of comparable thickness, and the large-size sheets eliminate the need for many joints and seams that would be necessary if regular boards were used. There is practically no shrinkage, expansion, or contraction, and the panels possess rigidity and strength in all directions. If well secured, they will not warp.

The production of plywood is normally divided between veneer construction and lumber-core construction. In veneer construction the faces run parallel to the length of the panel, with alternating plies at right angles; an odd number of plies (three, five, seven, etc.) is used. Lumbercore plywood has comparatively thick middle layer of solid wood, with a ⅟₁₆-inch layer on each side and a very thin face veneer (⅟₂₈ inch thick) outside. While more expensive than veneer-core plywood, it is ideal for projects like furniture, which call for doweled, splined, or dovetail joints.

Plywood is made with a moisture-resistant binder in the interior grades, while the exterior grade is waterproof. An almost endless variety of woods, from common fir to rare imported species, is used as the face or top veneer. The cost of the panel naturally depends upon the type of wood used as a face surface. Thicknesses range from ⅛ to 1 inch, the most common being ¼, ⅜, ½, ⅝, and ¾ inch. The standard sheet of plywood is 4 by 8 feet, but it is possible to obtain smaller or larger sheets when required.

HARDBOARD. Various compressed wood-pulp or hardboard products appear under many different trade names. These boards may often be used for the bottoms or backs of furniture or for the bottoms of drawers. Available in 4- by 8-foot sheets, ⅛ to ⅜ inch thick, hardboard is a dense, hard, grainless material, rich brown in color. It can be cut, nailed, and treated like any large thin wood panel. The sheets, composed of finely pulverized wood fibers mixed with a binder, are submitted to tremendous pressure to form a tough, moisture-resistant material. Hardboard takes a paint or wax finish very well.

ESTIMATING MATERIALS AND COSTS

Lumber is measured in various ways, depending upon the type of wood and its width and thickness. Lumber more than 4 inches wide and ½ to 2 inches thick is measured in board feet. A board foot is a square foot of lumber 1 inch thick. To figure the total board footage, multiply the thickness (nominal) of the board in inches by its width (nominal) and length in feet, or

$$\text{B.F.} = \text{thickness in inches} \times \frac{\text{width in inches}}{12} \times \text{length in feet}$$

Thus a piece of lumber 1 by 6 inches by 10 feet would measure 5 board feet—1x½x10 = 5. Lumber of this size is always quoted at a specified price per M (thousand) board feet. To find its cost: for example, if it was quoted at $120 per M board feet, it would be charged for at the rate of 12 cents per foot, and would cost 60 cents. The number of board feet in lumber of various sizes and lengths is shown in the Lumber Calculator below on opposite page.

Lumber less than 4 inches wide and of any thickness is frequently ordered by the linear foot. Thus, an order for a board 10 feet long would specify 10 linear feet.

Plywood and hardboard are ordered in square-foot measurements. A piece of plywood 4 by 8 feet equals 32 square feet.

When you order lumber, make a list of the number of boards you need, their sizes, types, and ultimate uses. From this list, add all lengths of lumber of similar wood, width, and thickness to get the total footage needed for each type.

You can then estimate costs by multiplying the price per board foot, linear foot, or square foot by the total footage needed. Because yard lumber is usually sold only in standard lengths, 15 per cent should be added to the estimated cost for the additional footage you may have to buy.

BASIC PROCEDURES

Making early American furniture can provide many hours of enjoyment for the members of your family. You can recruit them and put them to work in the assembly and finishing of the

LUMBER CALCULATOR—BOARD FEET FOR VARIOUS LENGTHS

SIZE IN INCHES	8-FOOT	10-FOOT	12-FOOT	14-FOOT	16-FOOT
1 x 2	1⅓	1⅔	2	2⅓	2⅔
1 x 3	2	2½	3	3½	4
1 x 4	2⅔	3⅓	4	4⅔	5⅓
1 x 5	3⅓	4⅙	5	5⅚	6⅔
1 x 6	4	5	6	7	8
1 x 8	5⅓	6⅔	8	9⅓	10⅔
1 x10	6⅔	8½	10	11⅔	13⅓
1 x12	8	10	12	14	16
1¼ *x 4	3⅓	4⅙	5	5⅚	6⅔
1¼ *x 6	5	6¼	7½	8¾	10
1¼ *x 8	6⅔	8⅓	10	11⅔	13⅓
1¼ *x10	8⅓	10⁵⁄₁₂	12½	14⁷⁄₁₂	16⅔
1¼ *x12	10	12½	15	17½	20
2 x 4	5⅓	6⅔	8	9⅓	10⅔
2 x 6	8	10	12	14	16
2 x 8	10⅔	13⅓	16	18⅔	21⅓
2 x10	13⅓	16⅔	20	23⅓	26⅔
2 x12	16	20	24	28	32

* Sometimes referred to as five-quarter boards.

pieces. It is important to realize, before starting any project, that good furniture cannot be made without accurate measurement, exact cutting and precision joining. Rushing a job may ruin many hours of hard work. It is best to plan the job completely and collect the necessary tools and materials before starting on a project.

In all woodworking projects you should follow these six major procedures:

1. Lay out the project by measuring, diagramming, and estimating the quantity of materials needed.

2. Mark the materials for length, width, and shape. Use a well-sharpened pencil, knife, or metal scriber for marking out lines. Be sure that the point of the pencil or scriber is as close to the edge of the rule or square as possible. The thickness of a blunt pencil can often mean the difference between a good fit and a poor one.

3. Cut the material to the exact size required.

Always make your cut on the outside, or waste side, of the line marked on the board. The blade of the saw has some thickness, and if you saw on the finish side, or inside, of the line or along the line itself, you may find that, in spite of your accuracy in measuring, the cut piece of wood is too short.

4. Join the cut parts into the desired assembly by nailing, screwing, or gluing and by using the most appropriate of the wide variety of joints available.

5. Prepare the surface for finishing.

6. Apply the finish material selected to give the project its final appearance.

To get the best results from any project, there are certain other fundamental principles that must be followed:

1. Be accurate when taking measurements and laying out work.

2. Lay out the job clearly by marking the dif-

ferent pieces—front, back, side, etc. Also mark all companion pieces where joints appear as 1 and 1, 2 and 2, etc.

3. Plan ahead as each step is completed.

4. Be orderly and neat. Take pride in turning out a fine job.

5. Use only the best materials. Since the difference in cost between good and cheap materials is small on a single project, it pays to buy the best.

6. All lumber must be squared, to find any deviation from a right angle, straight line, or plane surface, and it must be trued to the required size before proceeding with the actual work.

7. Joints must be made to fit together; never make them too loose or too tight. Remember, your finished item is only as strong as its weakest joint.

8. Wherever possible, duplicate pieces should be laid out and cut at the same time.

9. Keep all tools in good condition. A sharp blade or cutter makes work easier, safer, and more accurate.

Before starting any of the projects in Section II, be sure to carefully study the working drawing. This is your blueprint to all important dimensions as well as to how the furniture piece is to be assembled. In some cases, the working drawing also gives the shape of curved and scrolled parts by graphing the curve in squares of specified sizes. From this, a full-sized pattern can be laid out in squares to correct dimensions.

THE ART OF WOOD JOINERY

In Section II, various methods of wood joinery are illustrated. With each project, you may follow the technique illustrated or substitute almost any of the methods given here, depending on your woodworking skill and the tools available. *BUTT JOINT.* Perhaps the best method of wood joinery is the elementary butt joint. To fit a butt joint properly, proceed as follows:

1. Square the end of one piece of wood using a try square and pencil to mark all four sides.

2. Use a cross-cut or back saw to cut the wood along these lines.

3. Take the end just cut and set it against the piece of wood to which it will be fastened.

4. Secure the pieces together with glue, nails, screws or corrugated or other fasteners.

5. If an exceptionally strong joint is required, you can combine any of the previously mentioned methods or use them in conjunction with dowels, angle irons, mending plates or a T-strap. Even a combination of any of these methods with gluing will result in no more than about 25 per cent of the tensile strength of the wood parallel to the grain for holding power.

DOWEL JOINT. Actually the best way to make a butt joint is with dowels. The basic idea of this joint-fastener is to use a specially prepared dowel as a connecting pin between two wood parts— either edge-to-edge (as in forming a table top from boards), end-to-side (as in fitting a table rail to a leg), or end-to-edge (as in making a reinforced butt joint).

The dowels you use are special because they must be spiral-grooved in order to pass glue and air as they are inserted into the holes of the workpieces. They can be obtained, ready-grooved, at some lumber dealers, but do not bet on it. To groove your own dowels, simply pass the full length across a slightly-raised table saw blade (using the gate as a guide), twisting the shaft as you go. The groove need be only $\frac{1}{32}$-inch. When you cut up a supply of these pins, bevel both ends all around for easier handling at the insertion stage.

Dowels are usually made of hardwood, come in 3-foot lengths and in an assortment of diameters. When purchasing, inspect each one, eliminating any that are not true.

There are two methods used in doweling— the "open" method, and the "blind" method. In the open method, a hole is drilled completely through one piece of wood, and deeply into or through the one to be joined. The dowel is coated with glue and pushed completely through the drilled holes, joining the pieces, and the re-

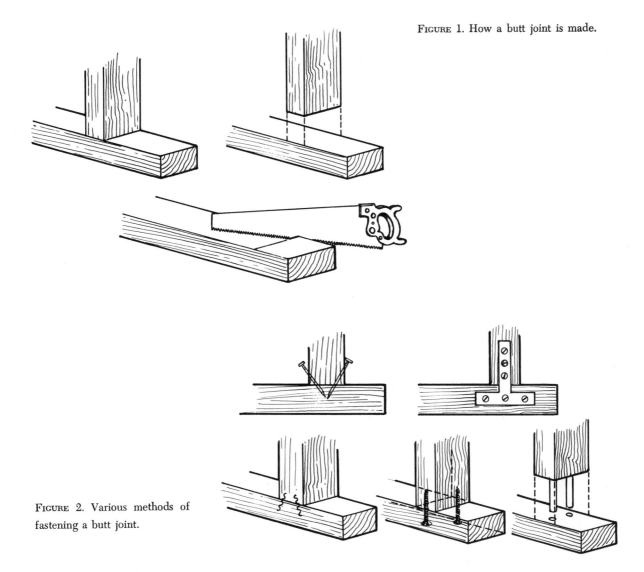

FIGURE 1. How a butt joint is made.

FIGURE 2. Various methods of fastening a butt joint.

mainder is sawed off flush with the outer surface.

In the blind method, holes are drilled part way into each piece from the joined faces, a dowel cut to the combined length of both holes. The dowel is then glue-coated and inserted in one hole and the second piece pressed onto the protruding dowel end. When using a blind dowel joint, keep these five basic rules in mind:

1. The diameter of the dowel used should be not less than ⅓ nor more than ½ the thickness of the boards to be joined.

2. The depth of the hole should be not less than ¼ nor more than ⅔ of the width of the nar-

rower board. A maximum depth of 4 inches is sufficient for 1 inch lumber and 8 inches for 2 inch lumber.

3. When drilling a hole near the end of a board, the hole should be at least the thickness of the board away from the end.

4. Always chamfer the ends of the dowels to prevent them from splitting when being inserted.

5. The total length of the dowel should be the combined depth of the two holes less ⅛ inch.

The trick in making a blind dowel joint is in the method for assuring exact alignment of the holes between the two workpieces. There are a

FIGURE 3. (A) Professional doweling machine is equipped with two fixed drills for producing aligned holes.

(B) Holes for dowel joints, as in photo A, are also made with portable drill, but this takes a lot of care.

(C) Spiral-groove your dowels by passing length across spinning blade, twisting the shaft as you go.

(D) Bevel the ends of individual dowels cut from shaft (photo C), apply glue and tap into holes with mallet.

(E) Finally joining two pieces, repeat the step in photo D.

(F) Clamp as you go—*never* omit clamping new joints, allowing more than ample time for glue to harden.

couple of devices which guarantee accurate results. All are variations of what is called the centering pin. For example, drill the holes in one workpiece, insert the little metal markers in the holes, and press the two workpieces together in the exact way they are to be assembled. The pins having made their indentations, you now have center points for the opposite set of holes. As an alternative some craftsmen use double-pointed thumb tacks to achieve the same results.

Another thing you want to be sure of when using a portable power drill, is producing a hole which is at right angles to the work surface. Aside from a steady, practiced hand, your best bet is to use a small glass level, taped to the housing, as a guide.

Apply plenty of glue (enough so that it squishes out of the work), and use clamps on every assembled component for at least 24 hours after gluing.

MORTISE-AND-TENON JOINT. The mortise-and-tenon is a mighty joint, stronger and more widely used than the dowel joint, and about the

best technique you can use in fine furniture making. You have probably seen the keyed mortise-and-tenon on heavy-stocked tables (where the tenon protrudes and a plug or wedge pierces it), but the blind mortise-and-tenon is much more widely used—and there would be no way of your knowing in this instance.

Essentially, the tenon is what is left of the end of one workpiece after cutting away part of two or four sides, and the mortise is the matching through-slot or blind pocket of the adjoining workpiece.

The big question to many beginning woodworkers is how to make the mortise. And to a lesser degree, the tenon—although equal care should be given both. Ideally, what you need for this joint-making is a table saw and a drill press with a hollow chisel mortising bit. The table saw will see you through exact tenons (a radial arm saw is good for only two of the four or four of the eight cuts that produce a tenon), and the mortising bit will cut square corners and straight sides for a blind pocket or through-slot in no time

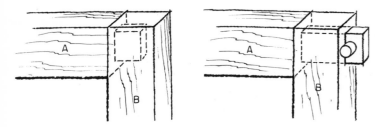

FIGURE 4. Two common types of mortise and tenon joints used in early American furniture.

at all. If you do not have this kind of equipment, hand tools will do. But they will take longer and you will really have to watch yourself.

Tenons are easily produced with a back saw, notching two sides of one end, or four sides, as the case may be. Mortises can be made with a chisel and mallet all the way, or with a chisel

for finishing off a mortise started with a brace-and-bit.

Making the tenon cuts on a table saw is very systematized. Assuming you are working with ¾-inch framing stock on a furniture project, you will want a ⁵⁄₁₆-inch tenon. All you have to do is set up with two blades separated by a ⁵⁄₁₆-inch spacer, and run the stock through to the depth (or length) you want—usually, a 1¾-inch tenon if you are working with a 2-inch framing. Cut off the scrap later, using one blade on the machine. If you do not have a spacer or you have only one blade, you can still make the basic cuts, one at a time.

Joining the mortise and the tenon, apply plenty of glue, and nail the pieces together with sash nails (they have no heads), finally clamping.

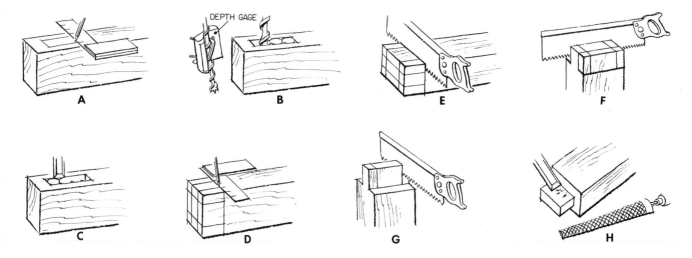

FIGURE 5. How to cut a mortise and tenon with hand tools:

(A) Measure and mark location of mortise using a square to make certain of perfect alignment.

(B) With brace and bit drill series of holes in area. For blind mortise, use a depth gage for proper depth.

(C) Clean excess wood cut of mortise with a sharp chisel. Make sure corners are cut square and are even.

(D) Mark tenon, drawing all lines square with edge of board. Mark on all sides to avoid error.

(E) Use back saw to "shoulder" of tenon. Cut across a board first to exact depth, keeping saw perfectly aligned.

(F) Turn board in vise and cut down edge to the two points cut in previous step to form a square corner.

(G) The other parts, called "cheeks," are cut in the same manner as the wide sections. Add guidelines before cutting.

(H) With sharp chisel and file, smooth surfaces of the tenon and check fit in mortise. Sandpaper smooth afterward.

FIGURE 6. How to cut a mortise and tenon with power tools:

Make a mortise-and-tenon joint using this special bit in drill press—or hand chisel.

Make a tenon on table saw using two blades separated by a spacer—or single blade in two passes.

Run the workpiece through the blades in one pass; depth of this cut will be about 1-1/4" (standard).

Switch to a single blade if necessary and make cross-cut, notching each side, producing the tenon.

FIGURE 6, CONTINUED
This is what the finished tenon looks like; chamfer the end of tenon all around for an easier fit.

Apply glue to mortise and tenon, join them, drive sash nails to strengthen and clamp the joint.

DADO JOINT. The dado joint is no more than a groove, called a dado, into which the end or side of a companion piece is fitted. It is remarkably practical, workmanlike and easy to make, being a favorite joint for shelf construction, bookcases, and drawers.

Time was, you would make two cuts across the grain—representing the overall thickness of the piece to be joined—with a back saw, then chisel out the groove. This would require constant checks with a depth gauge, to make sure the groove was flat at the bottom.

There is nothing to stop you from this hand-worked approach, however, despite power tools. With the portable circular saw set to the necessary depth, the two outside or limit cuts are made first, then the area between is reduced by repeated passes of the single blade. This can also be accomplished with a radial arm saw and a table saw, the latter being a tricky method because of working upside down.

The dado adapter or dado blade set is the smart way to fast dado grooves. Consisting of two outside blades and one, two, three or four inside cutters (depending on how wide you want your groove), the dado can be made in one pass or swipe of the blades. As a guide, when using ¾-inch stock, a groove of ¾-inch is standard.

When assembling, glue the entire joint, and hold workpieces together with a bar clamp. Drive nails or screws and countersink them, patching the holes.

MITER JOINT. Primarily the miter joint is for show—when, for example, you want uninterrupted wood grain around edges (side-to-top-to-side of a cabinet) or at corners (a picture frame). The joining ends or edges are usually cut at angles of 45 degrees, then glued, clamped and nailed. Cuts slightly less than 45 degrees are often necessary when fitting new moldings on settled window casings, but the differences are

FIGURE 7. How to cut a dado:

ABOVE: Dado blade set makes the perfect dado or groove in one pass, eliminating the extra step in photo above right.

ABOVE RIGHT: If you have no dado blades, you can produce the necessary groove with one blade in series of passes.

RIGHT: Partially completed dado cut shows how one blade in repeated passes has begun to remove waste stock.

hardly noticeable, once they are up and painted.

One thing is for sure, there is a definite finished look to a mitered joint, whether it is left natural or painted. The planning of the cut and the assembly of the joint, however, need more care than the actual cutting. What with the miter box for molding or trim stock and the radial arm saw for sheet work, as well, the cuts are highly sys-tematized. And to scribe a 45-degree angle on your work, all you have to use is a combination square, try square, miter square or bevel as a preset, sure guide. Assembly can be heartbreak-ing though, unless you control your work every step of the way. The joining of the two ends or sides must be precise, neat and trim—and add up to an exact 90-degree turn.

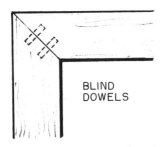 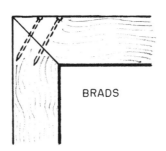 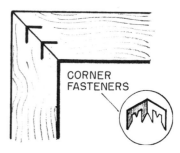

BLIND DOWELS

BRADS

CORNER FASTENERS

FIGURE 8. Three common ways of fastening a miter joint.

On corner work involving molding or trim pieces, use miter corner clamps specially made for the purpose. These devices assure a square set after you have glued.

Assembling sheet stock (i.e., long, mitered sides), you will find that handling and squaring of the parts is made easier with a spline: After making your miter cuts, a groove is then cut into each edge, at right angles to the bevel, and a wood strip (the spline) is ripped to fit the double groove as the mitered edges are brought together, forming a corner. Reinforced in this manner, the miter joint is many times stronger. You can use the same technique in a different correlation of the parts—or you can use corrugated nails where it is practical.

In every instance of mitered construction, always use corner clamps, web clamping devices or plain old rope to hold your workpiece in square when drying. Mitered articles, more than any other jointed project, have a tendency to shift without your knowing it, so you have got to keep a sharp eye.

RABBET JOINT. The rabbet joint is like a dado except that it has only two surfaces (a bottom and one side) and therefore has to be made at the edge of your workpiece (unlike the rabbet, the dado occurs anywhere, except along an edge).

In making a drawer, for example, rabbet joints are extremely practical, allowing sides jointed at the ends of faces (recessed sides would have to be dado-jointed). You have also seen rabbet cuts (not rabbet joints) used as lips on kitchen cabinet doors.

The cleanest, quickest way to cut a rabbet is with a dado head. Or you can use a notching technique with a single blade—on a radial arm or bench saw (see the photo sequence). When ready to assemble, glue well, nail and clamp the parts for 24 hours.

LAP JOINT. Bring two workpieces together, notch them equally where they overlap and you have got either a cross-lap joint, a half-lap joint (end-to-end, at right angles) or a tee half-lap (end-to-side, at right angles). The desired visual effect, of course, is that the two thicknesses overlap within a single thickness's tolerance.

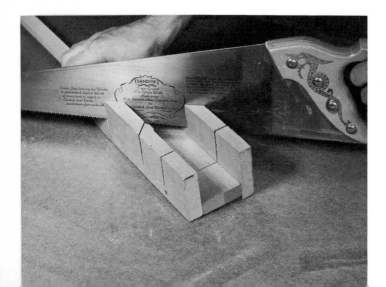

FIGURE 9. To cut a miter by hand, use a miter box as shown at the left.

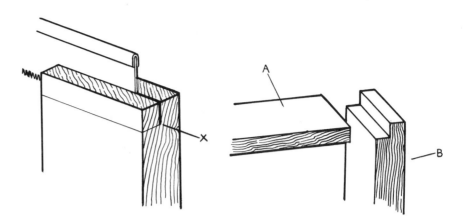

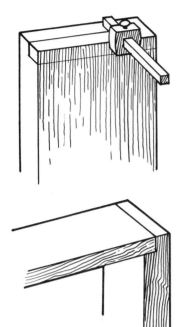

FIGURE 10. How to make a rabbet joint with hand tools: Make certain that ends of both pieces are square. Then take piece B and with try square make line across; the distance from the end of the board is the thickness of piece. Next, using marking gauge, draw a line across the end of piece B. This distance is one-third or one-half the thickness. Then, using back saw, cut along line of the board's end to the depth of the drawn line, point X. Next, using the same saw, now cut along the other line to meet first cut. Then place boards in position and fasten.

FIGURE 11. How to make a rabbet joint with power tools:

RIGHT: Making a rabbet cut on table saw, first put very firm pressure against the fence, make cut across grain as shown.

BELOW: Having adjusted the fence for the second pass, turn the workpiece on end and cut away the scrap to form rabbet.

LOWER RIGHT: Glue the component pieces (one side is the rabbeted stock) and clamp firmly, making sure to check for square.

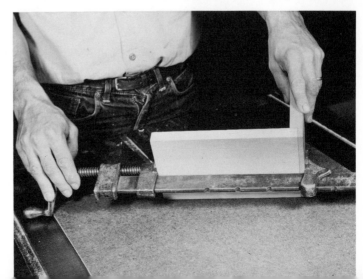

FIGURE 12. To make the cross-lap joint, mark the workpiece (stock next to fence is guide only) and make the two limit cuts.

Now remove the scrap between the two limit cuts by jockeying work beneath saw, taking successive bites.

The finished lap cuts look like this; their inner surfaces serrated by the repeated passes of the saw blade.

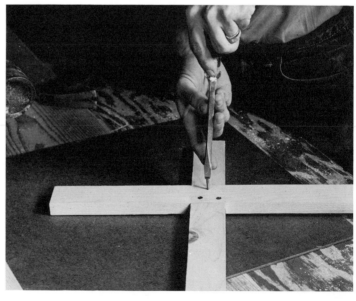

The cross-lap joint is glued and screwed, the two pieces now overlapping one another within a single thickness.

Grooving for the lap is simple enough with power. A bench saw, radial arm saw or portable circular saw equipped with a dado head will clear the necessary grooves in no time. Just remember to limit your dado passes to a ¼-inch depth-of-cut at a time. For instance, a 1-inch groove in 2-inch stock should take you four passes—never overload the dado head with any deeper cut. As for the width of any groove you make, there is no limit. All you have to do is keep repeating the basic cut until you are finished.

You can, of course, make the grooves with a single blade in repeated passes; i.e., the measure of the blade's kerf divided into the width of the groove. Without power, you can make your two limit cuts with a back saw, then chip out the stock between with a chisel—in which case, use a depth gauge as you near the bottom of the groove, checking for an even, flat bottom surface.

The fit of the two pieces should be snug. Also, test for surface evenness of the lap with a steel straightedge. Preparatory to assembling, drill pilot holes for the screws, then glue and clamp the parts, inserting the screws after the lap has been positioned.

DOVETAIL JOINT. The interlocking of two pieces of wood by special fan-shaped cutting is called a dovetail joint. It is used extensively by skilled craftsmen in making fine furniture, drawers and in projects where good appearance and strength are desired. A dovetail joint has considerable strength because of the flare of the projections, technically known as pins, on the ends of the boards, which fit exactly into similarly shaped dovetails. The spaces between the dovetails and the spaces between the pins are called mortises or sockets. The dovetails are visible on the face or flat side of one of the pieces being joined and the pins are visible on the end of the other piece.

Dovetail joints are made in a variety of ways. A major breakdown can be made according to appearance:

1. Through dovetails are joints where the dovetail and pin are clearly visible from two sides of the joint.

2. Stopped dovetails or half-blind dovetails are

FIGURE 13. Cutting dovetails with hand tools can be a lengthy task.

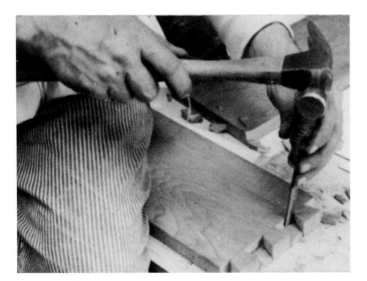

joints where the face of one board is perfectly smooth and the pins and dovetails are visible on the face of the other.

3. Blind dovetail joints are those where all the cutting is done without marring the outside face of either of the two pieces.

Cutting dovetail joints calls for precision craftsmanship. They can be cut by hand using a dovetail saw and small chisel or with a special template or pattern with a router. The latter is highly accurate and considerably faster than cutting by hand.

Handymen who own a radial arm saw can make a modified dovetail joint sometimes called a finger joint. It is easy to cut with this type of a saw. Actually, to cut this joint, the saw arbor has to be tilted so that the blade is parallel to the table top. After a saw cut is made by pulling the saw out along the arm, the blade is pushed back and the entire motor, arbor and blade are lowered or raised, depending upon whether you

started making the cuts at the base or top of the board. It is sometimes necessary to support the board being cut so that it does not rest directly on the table. As long as one face of the board rests against the table fence, you will encounter no difficulty in cutting this joint.

Perhaps the most direct way to a dovetail is the dovetail kit, useful to you as an accessory if you own a router. One kit, for example, makes joints in stock from 7/16-inch to 1 inch and contains (1) a 7/16-inch template guide, (2) a dovetail fixture, (3) a finger template and (4) a 9/16-inch dovetail bit. Working with thinner stock—from 5/16-inch to 5/8-inch—there is still another kit containing (1) a dovetail fixture, (2) a smaller finger template, (3) a 5/16-inch template guide, and (4) a 9/32-inch dovetail bit.

ADHESIVES AND GLUES

At one time when we spoke of glue we meant a product derived from an organic material such as animal hide, bones or hoofs. Its primary use was for bonding wood, leather, paper and similar porous materials. The word adhesive on the other hand, was used to describe synthetic materials produced from man-made plastics or resins which could often be used on non-porous materials as well. In recent years, however, the terms "glue" and "adhesive" are used almost interchangeably. While there are still some made entirely of organic products, most glues have a synthetic plastic or resin base and can be used on a great many materials.

The following are the more popular furniture making glues on the market today:

LIQUID ANIMAL GLUE is a high strength organic glue excellent for general woodworking applications where strength is required, but where little or no dampness will be encountered. You can use it on wood, leather, cork and similar porous materials. This glue is exceptionally resistant to heat and mold. In color, it is light brown or amber and will help to fill small gaps and rough areas in poorly fitted joints. Full

FIGURE 14. Cutting dovetails with a radial arm saw.

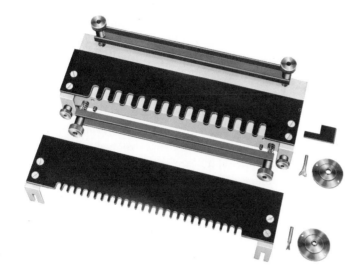

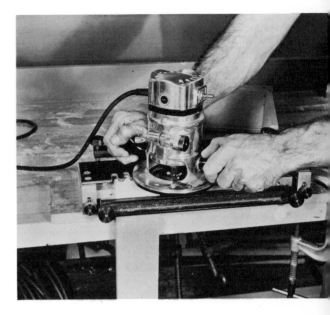

FIGURE 15.

TOP LEFT: Components of dovetail kit are shown, including alternate finger template, for joints 7/16" to 1".

TOP RIGHT: Router is a work shaping the characteristic dovetails, following the fingers of the template as guide.

LEFT: Two component pieces are shown, dovetailed and ready for assembling.

clamping pressure is required while setting; clamps can be removed after about one hour. Since this glue tends to thicken at low temperatures, you may have to warm it to facilitate spreading if you are working some place where it is less than 70 degrees.

CASEIN GLUE is a powdered wood glue for heavy duty work where strong joints are required.

It is mixed with water before each use, and is the only woodworking glue that can be used in cold weather in an unheated workshop—or even outdoors down to the freezing point. It is also ideal for poorly fitted or loose joints since the glue tends to fill voids and gaps better than most types. Only moderate clamping pressure is needed but this glue is not waterproof and may stain some dark or acid woods. It is excellent, however, for oily, hard-to-glue woods such as teak, yew or lemonwood.

PLASTIC RESIN GLUE is the thing to use when a really strong and highly water-resistant wood glue is needed. Excellent for high grade furniture work and cabinet construction, its bonds are actually stronger than the wood itself. It is chemically neutral so will not stain acid woods such as oak or mahogany. Room temperatures—70 degrees or warmer—are a must, and for maximum strength, joints must be smooth and accurately fitted. Firm clamping pressure for at least 10 hours insures a good bond. Plastic resin glues are also highly resistant to mold and rot and when properly applied will leave little or no glue line to mar the finished appearance.

RESORCINOL GLUE is completely waterproof. Though the plastic resin glues just described are also highly water-resistant the two-component resorcinol type is better for a project where a completely waterproof glue is a definite requirement. Consisting of a powdered resin and a separate catalyst which must be mixed together, this is the glue to use for outdoor furniture, boats or anything that needs the strongest waterproof joint. Like the single-component plastic resins, this glue also must be used at room temperature (70 degrees or over) and it, too, requires firm clamping pressure for at least 10 hours. Since all plastic resin glues tend to shrink as they dry, joints must be smooth and snug fitting with no gaps or open spaces. This glue hardens by chemical interaction of the two components, rather than by air-drying; temperature must be maintained at 70 degrees or higher while the joint is curing. If it drops the glue will dry anyway, but the joint will be much weaker.

CONTACT CEMENT has as its principal characteristic, as indicated by its name, the property of bonding on contact without clamping. Its principal use is for bonding plastic laminates to counter tops, table tops and similar flat surfaces, but it is also ideal for bonding leather, linoleum, thin gauge metal and many other dissimilar materials, where clamping pressure is impossible or difficult to apply. The cement is applied to both surfaces, then allowed to dry for about 30 minutes before the parts are pressed together. Once you bring the two cement-coated surfaces in contact, they bond instantly; they cannot be shifted around to line them up. Most brands are highly inflammable, but there are new nonflammable varieties which are much safer. Though contact cement will bond wood, as well as many other materials, the joints are not really strong enough for woodworking.

Contact cement-coated surfaces will not stick to anything but other similarly coated surfaces. Use "slip sheets" of wrapping paper between the parts being bonded while aligning them. Then, when everything is lined up, slowly slide the sheet of paper out of the way while pressing the two coated surfaces together.

APPLYING GLUES. Remember that the manufacturer's directions will give you the best possible results—so take time out to familiarize yourself with them before you start.

Regardless of which glue or adhesive you select, remember that there are certain rules to observe if you want to be sure of long-lasting permanent results. Surfaces to be bonded should be clean; remove all dust, moisture, wax and grease beforehand.

When working with a glue that has to be mixed before use, make certain to measure ingredients carefully, then take the time to mix them thoroughly. This is particularly true with the two-part synthetic resins. Thorough blending is required to start the chemical reaction that makes them harden. With some, temperature limitations must also be carefully adhered to. Using these at temperatures well below recommended limits may not necessarily interfere with their hardening, but it will greatly weaken the resulting bond.

One more important point to remember is that all porous surfaces need special treatment. Spread a thin coat of glue on both surfaces to be joined, let it stand until tacky. This first coat will dry partly by evaporation, partly by being drawn into the pores of the material. Spread on the second coat and join, then clamp in place.

When preparing wood for gluing, remember that shrinkage and a tendency to warp are greatest at the ends of the pieces. To join long pieces take an extra shaving from the middle section so that greater pressure will be applied at the ends by the clamps. Flat boards should be glued together with the sap sides back to back to equalize the strain of this warpage tendency. Boards glued side by side to form wider boards should have heart and sap sides turned up alternately so warpage will be held to a wavy pattern rather than bowing from outer edges.

Engineers will tell you that two surfaces can be made so smooth that they will cling together more tightly than any adhesive can bind them. Such perfection cannot be expected in the home, but you should come as close to it as possible. It takes but a few seconds to turn a poor fit into a good one. When glue is added, the material will then be so well joined, the joint will be stronger than the materials themselves.

Neatness in all gluing is essential. Wipe away excess glue with a cloth dipped in water if you work with animal or casein glue: wipe while glue is still moist. Plastic glue can be wiped up with acetone (nail polish is a form of this substance). Waterproof glue can be cleaned up with alcohol.
CLAMPS AND CLAMPING. In practically all woodwork, you need a vise in which to clamp your stock. But regardless of the type of vise you use, you should also have clamps to hold stock which cannot be worked in your vise.

There are many different types of clamps but virtually all are used for the same purpose—to hold two pieces of work together for convenience or during the drying of an adhesive. Among the clamps which the handyman might use in his workshop are:

1. Most commonly used in the workshop is a C-clamp. It comes in a number of sizes and types.

2. Hand screws are fine woodworking clamps and have wooden jaws that are parallel with each other. They can be used to clamp work that is flat or wedge-shaped. Machinists' clamps are similar in design, but are smaller and made of steel.

3. Bar clamps are used by the craftsman. They are long precision clamps normally used for fine furniture making.

4. Pipe clamps, however, are often used by the handyman in place of bar clamps. These are available to fit either ½-inch or ¾-inch diameter iron pipe. Only one end of the pipe need be threaded. The handyman should have several different lengths of pipe to use with his clamps. While you can use a long pipe for all jobs, the excess pipe might get in your way. It is always best to use pipe clamps, like bar clamps, in pairs.

5. Special clamps are made to hold pieces of wood at right angles while they are being joined.

FIGURE 16. Two types of bar clamps used by furniture makers.

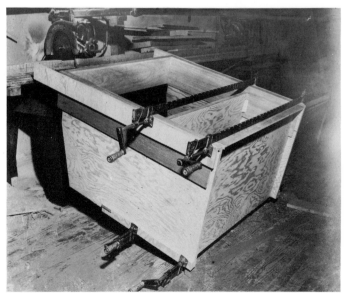

Many of these have openings in their sides through which you can insert nails or screws.

6. C-plier clamps are handy adjustable clamps for small work.

It is possible to make your own clamps for securing work. For instance, a homemade wedge clamp is excellent for binding boards that are to be glued together, edge to edge. It is easy to make and use, as shown in the drawing here. Here is how it is done:

1. Construct this clamp from scrap lumber ¾ to 1 inch thickness, 6 to 8 inches wide and about one-half as long as the boards to be glued. On the wide side of the clamp material, mark each end at the midpoint from the sides. Now measure up and mark a point ½ inch above the center on one end and on the other end ½ inch below. Connect these two points by a diagonal line and saw through the material lengthwise along the line. This will give you two wedge-shaped pieces of the required angle, regardless of the length of the material.

2. Apply glue to both contact edges of the boards to be glued and place these edges in the correct permanent position on a level wood surface, over waxed paper, and against a backboard or butt.

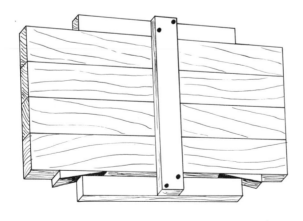

FIGURE 17. A simple clamping arrangement to hold boards together for edge-to-edge gluing.

3. Drive a nail that is about one and one-half times longer than the thickness of the wedges into, but not through, one of the wedges only, on the flat surface near each end, as shown in the drawing.

4. Put the wedges together as sawed, having on the outside and near the middle of the board the one into which the nails were driven, the other one against the outside edge of the board to be clamped.

5. Then drive the nails partly through into the surface below, deeply enough to hold the outer wedge firmly in place but leaving the nail heads above the surface in order that they may be pulled out easily later.

6. Pound the inner wedge tightly in place from the wider end, creating a strong tension against the glued boards. If the boards to be glued are thin, it will be necessary to place a weight on them to keep them from buckling.

7. Using a damp cloth, wipe off any excess glue squeezed out on the upper surface and keep the boards clamped for 48 hours. A knife may be used later to clear the bottom side of any excess glue. When using wedge clamps, remember that the work must be done on a level, clean surface, such as a workbench with a back wall to butt against. A section of a wood floor adjoining a wall is an excellent spot, provided you do not object to nail holes in the flooring.

HOW TO USE CLAMPS. To the standard woodworking, keep these facts in mind:

1. To protect the surface of the work, it is best to place a thin hardwood board between the clamp face and the work.

2. Use clamps in pairs on both ends of the work. This will prevent one end from separating while the other is being joined. For large surfaces, additional clamps are needed.

3. Apply even pressure on all clamps. Tighten as far as possible by hand. After a few minutes, take a few extra turns on the clamp handle, if possible. However, avoid pressing in the sides of the work.

4. Keep clamps in proper working condition.

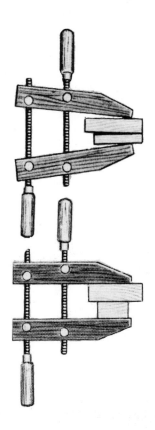

FIGURE 18. Hand screws require care in applying pressure. Turn both screws at once.

Keep the screw sections well oiled, remove any burs from the face and prevent rust from forming on any part of the clamp.

SCREWS AND NAILS

There are two basic fastening devices employed in early American furniture projects given in Section II. They are, of course, nails and screws.

NAILING. The length, diameter, head size, and approximate number to a pound of the various penny sizes of common nails and finishing nails are given on page 36.

A nail must be properly selected for the work it is to do so that it will not split the wood or

distort the fibers. The type of nail that distorts the fibers of the wood the least will have the greatest holding power.

In fastening hardwoods, bore holes slightly smaller than the diameter of the nail and to a depth two-thirds of its length. In nailing a board end, blunt the tip of the nail to prevent it from splitting the end. A few staggered nails are stronger than a large number of nails in a row. If one of two pieces of wood to be joined is thin, use nails that will penetrate one-half to three-quarters of the second piece.

Corrugated fasteners, often called "wiggle nails," are used for holding two wood surfaces together side by side. They can be used for making window screens, screen doors, window frames, flower boxes, etc., and for tightening loose joints or cracks in woodwork. They are made with a plain edge for hardwoods and a saw edge for softwoods. They are generally used with glue for better holding power.

There is a trick in driving a corrugated fastener. Use a medium-weight hammer and strike light blows that are evenly distributed over the outside edge. It is essential that the pieces being fastened together rest on something solid while the fastener is driven in.

Another steel fastener, the clamp nail, is new in woodworking. These nails are used on miter joints only. The wide end of the clamp nail is driven into a saw cut $\frac{5}{16}$ inch deep on both edges of the miter, and the joint is held more firmly than with corrugated fasteners.

In fine work where the nailhead must not show or must be inconspicuous, it is driven well below the surface with a nail set. The hole in the wood over the nailhead can then be filled flush with the surface with putty, plastic wood, or sawdust mixed with glue.

Nail sets are made in several sizes, usually $\frac{1}{32}$, $\frac{2}{32}$, and $\frac{4}{32}$ inch, the size being indicated by the diameter of the small end of the tapered shank. The end of a nail set is often "cupped" or hollowed, which prevents it from "walking" or slipping on the nail. Use a nail set of a size which

COMMON NAILS

SIZE	LENGTH	DIAMETER GAUGE NO.	DIAMETER OF HEAD	APPROX. NO. PER POUND
2d	1″	15	11/64″	830
3d	1¼″	14	13/64″	528
4d	1½″	12½	¼″	316
5d	1¾″	12½	¼″	271
6d	2″	11½	17/64″	168
7d	2¼″	11½	17/64″	150
8d	2½″	10¼	9/32″	106
9d	2¾″	10¼	9/32″	96
10d	3″	9	5/16″	69
12d	3¼″	9	5/16″	63
16d	3½″	8	11/32″	49
20d	4″	6	13/32″	31

FINISHING NAILS

SIZE	LENGTH	DIAMETER GAUGE NO.	DIAMETER OF HEAD GAUGE NO.	APPROX. NO. PER POUND
2d	1″	16½	13½	1351
3d	1¼″	15½	12½	807
4d	1½″	15	12	584
5d	1¾″	15	12	500
6d	2″	13	10	309
8d	2½″	12½	9½	189
10d	3″	11½	8½	121
16d	3½″	11	8	90
20d	4″	10	7	62

will not enlarge the hole made by the head of the nail.

FIGURE 19. Nails and screws both should be countersunk and the hole filled with the wood dough or surfacing putty. It is recommended that the filler be applied so that it is slightly higher than the wood, then sanded level when dry.

SCREWING. Screws have much greater holding power than nails. Another advantage: work held together by them is easily taken apart and put together again without damaging the pieces.

A little soap rubbed into the threads of a wood screw makes it easier to drive.

If a screw is driven in without first boring a pilot hole for the threaded part, the wood may split, and in some instances the screwhead may be twisted off. Bore holes for small screws with a small brad awl, for large screws with bits or twist drills. If the wood is soft (pine, spruce, basswood, etc.), bore the hole only about half as deep as the threaded part of the screw. If the wood is hard (oak, maple, birch, etc.), the hole must be almost as deep as the screw.

If the screw is large or if it is a brass screw, bore a pilot hole slightly smaller in diameter than the threaded part of the screw and then enlarge the hole at the top with a second drill of the same diameter as the unthreaded portion of the screw.

When two pieces of wood are to be fastened tightly together with screws, two sets of holes must be drilled. The holes are drilled so that the threaded portion of the screw "bites" or takes hold only in the under piece of wood. The piece on top is clamped to the lower piece by the pressure of the screwhead. There are five steps in the operation:

1. Locate the position of the screw holes and mark them with a brad awl. The awl mark will center the drill and prevent it from "walking" away with the spot.

2. Bore a pilot hole, slightly smaller in diameter than the threaded portion of the screw, all the way through the upper piece of wood and into the lower piece half the length of the threaded part of the screw.

3. Enlarge the pilot hole in the upper piece of wood by drilling it out to the same diameter as (or slightly larger than) the shank or unthreaded portion of the screw.

BODY AND LEAD HOLES FOR WOOD SCREWS

SCREW GAUGE	BODY HOLE DRILL NO.	PILOT HOLE DRILL NO.	COUNTERSINK DRILL NO.
0	53	Unnecessary	32
1	49	Unnecessary	20
2	44	56	16
3	40	56	4
4	33	52	B
5	⅛	52	F
6	28	47	L
7	24	47	O
8	19	42	S
9	15	42	T
10	10	42	X
11	5	38	$7/16$
12	$7/32$	38	$29/64$
14	D	31	$33/64$
16	I	28	$37/64$
18	$19/64$	23	$41/64$

4. If flathead or ovalhead screws are to be used, countersink the clearance hole in the upper piece of wood to match the diameter of the heads of the screws. If roundhead screws or cup washers are used, do not countersink.

5. Drive all screws firmly in place and, after they are all in, tighten each of them.

HOW TO CONCEAL SCREW HEADS. Finishing nails should be used so that the heads may be set below the surface of the wood and the small holes filled with wood putty. The heads of screws should also be concealed. It is best, therefore, to use flathead screws, unless otherwise called for in specific plans.

The head of the flathead screw can be concealed if a countersink bit is used when making the pilot holes for screws. Here are several ways in which flathead screws can be used:

1. The screw head can be driven so that the top is flush with the surface of the wood. This is all right for a back panel, but most people do not like to see the exposed head of a flathead screw.

2. The head can be driven deeper into the wood and the hole above it filled with wood filler to conceal the head.

3. However, most wood fillers are difficult to finish so that they do not stand out from the rest of the surface. Therefore, a hole large enough

to receive the head of the screw is bored deep enough to provide for a plug. The wood plug can be made out of a dowel or cut out of the same wood stock as the surface with a plug cutter. The plug is secured with adhesive. You can, if you use the same wood to make the plugs, set the plugs in so that the grain runs in the same direction as the surface or at right angles to it.

4. Another method of concealing the head of the screw is to use wood screw-hole buttons. These are similar to plugs, but they have a rounded or oval top surface and some also have a distinct head. They extend slightly above the surface of the wood and can be obtained in matching or contrasting hardwoods.

HOW TO JOIN BOARDS

Many of the early American pieces described in this book require wide boards. Unfortunately it is not always possible to get boards of these widths. While it is possible to use plywood, you may prefer to use solid lumber. There are several ways in which to join boards to obtain one large one.

1. The straight butt joint is one of the simplest and most frequently used. All boards are jointed, that is, the edges planed so that they are square

FIGURE 20.

LEFT TO RIGHT: The tongue-and-groove-joint, the feather or spline joint, and the modified tongue-and-groove joint.

with the face or flat side of the board. Adhesive is applied along the edges and the boards are locked together with clamps until the adhesive has set.

2. Rabbet joints are more difficult to make and, therefore, less frequently used. To make this joint, it is necessary to joint all boards and then cut a rabbet on each edge, except for the outside edges of the first and last board. The individual boards are secured with adhesive and clamps.

3. Dowel joining of individual pieces to make one large board is used often, especially with large surfaces. A blind dowel technique is employed to join the boards edge to edge (see page 18).

4. Tongue-and-groove joints are practical only if you have a shaper or shaper attachment to cut the tongue and groove along the edges of each board. The pieces are joined with adhesives and clamps.

5. The feather joint or spline technique is one of the most practical ways to join individual, small boards. This joint requires the use of power tools. Each cut has to be exact and hardwood must be used for the "feathers" or "splines." Again, it is necessary to use adhesive and clamps.

6. A modified tongue-and-groove technique can be used. The ends of the boards are cut with a tongue and a narrow end piece or cleat is cut with a groove. This transverse rail, which runs at right angles to the boards, tends to eliminate any tendency toward warping. It is fastened with adhesives to the boards and adhesive is also used between the edges of the boards.

HOW TO JOIN A CORNER

The simplest corner technique is the butt joint where one piece fits flush against the other. However, the butt joint offers the least amount of strength and should be substituted with one of the following whenever possible and applicable:

A. Although the end lap joint is easy to make, it is rarely found in good furniture. The joint is often reinforced with screws, or even bolts, plus adhesive.

B. Dowel joints are fairly common and frequently used to attach a leg to a frame. While the dowels can be driven in from the outside edge, it is best to use the blind doweling technique for furniture making.

C. A through mortise and tenon is often used by the handyman but less frequently found in professionally built furniture. This joint is easy to make with a power saw with a dado head.

D. The open mortise and tenon looks more professional and is stronger than the through mortise and tenon. The mortise can be cut with a mortising chisel on a drill press.

E. The conventional mitered joint with its 45 degree angle is not advised for any corner which will be subject to unusual strain or excessive weights. This joint is best to use on trim around cabinet doors and elsewhere, rather than at the primary corners of the furniture piece.

F. A miter joint with a spline, which is much stronger, can be made by the amateur. The joint is cut in the regular manner, then a groove is cut in each end and a spline inserted. Secure with adhesive.

G. A rabbet is frequently used for joining the top of a piece of furniture to the sides. Whether cut in the side piece or the top piece, the rabbet leaves only a narrow strip of end grain visible.

H. A box corner is sometimes used when making furniture, but the handyman is advised against this type of a joint since there is always a strong possibility of cracks along the edges.

I. A mitered rabbet joint is easy to make with a power saw and looks professional. The pieces may be secured with dowels, screws or nails in addition to adhesive.

J. A lock miter joint is one of the better types for the experienced handyman to use when making furniture. The pieces must be cut accurately on a power saw. They are held securely with adhesive.

K. A milled corner joint is used extensively in

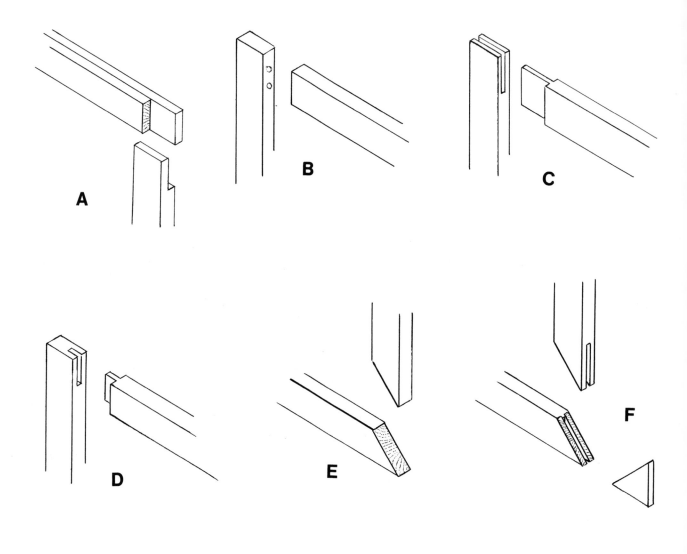

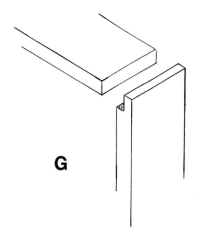

FIGURE 21. Various ways of joining a corner. Letters correspond to those in the text.

the making of drawers. It is much stronger than the box corner joint and less subject to cracking; it has closed edges.

L. A half-blind dovetail joint is not recommended for the handyman without power tools. This joint is often used when making drawers and is very strong when held with adhesive.

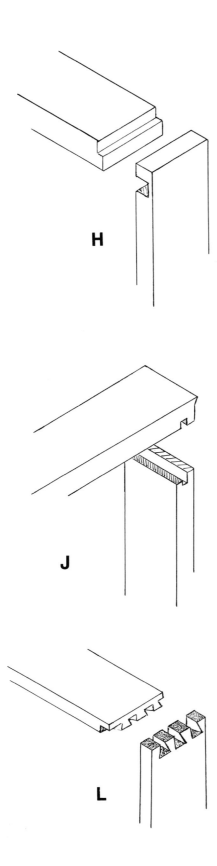

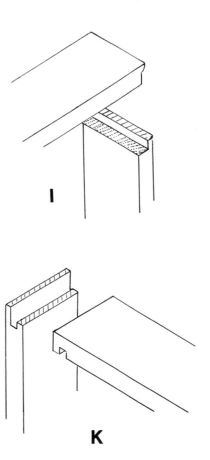

HOW TO ADD CENTER BOARDS

Certain projects in Section II require shelves or center support boards. Here are four ways to do this job:

A. For a butt joint cut the shelf or center board to fit between the two sides. The board is then secured with nails or screws and adhesive. This type of a joint is not very strong and will not support any extensive weight.

B. A dado joint is much stronger and looks more workmanlike. The dado can be cut with a dado head on a power saw, a dado plane, a back saw, chisel and mallet or with a router. The center board or shelf is held with adhesive and, if necessary, countersink screws or counterset nails.

C. A stopped dado joint is more difficult to make by hand. It looks better than the ordinary

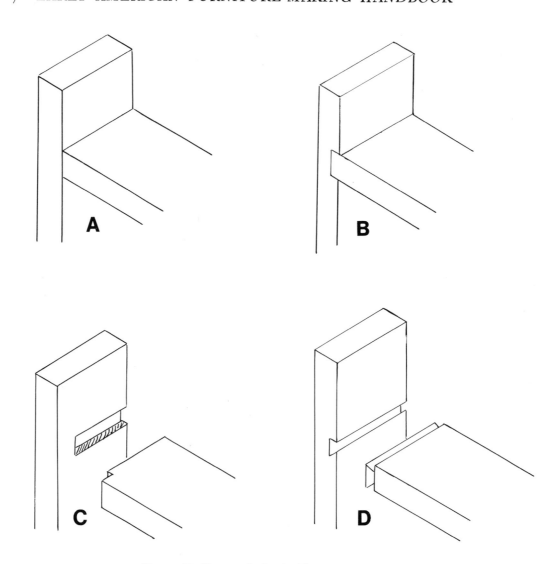

FIGURE 22. Four methods of adding a center board.

dado for the front edge of the side upright is uncut. It combines the finished appearance of a butt joint with the strength of a dado joint.

D. A dovetail slip joint is exceedingly strong and is best cut with a power saw. If this method is used, there is little chance of the sides pulling apart.

ADJUSTABLE SHELVES. Often, it is best to have the shelves adjustable so that they can be varied depending upon your needs. Here are three simple ways to do the job:

1. Dowel pin method involves drilling a series of holes parallel to the edge of the upright and the insertion of a short length of dowel below the shelf. Normally, a ⅜-inch dowel should be used for a moderate-size shelf, but the exact size depends upon the length of the shelf and the weight it will support.

2. In place of the dowel pin, there are special metal spade pins which fit into predrilled holes. These metal supports are available in specialty hardware stores.

3. Another method of obtaining adjustable shelves is to use adjustable shelf standards and supports. It is necessary to use a pair of standards on each side of the shelf and four supports are

used for each shelf. This hardware is carried by specialty stores.

HOW TO ADD PANELS

Panels are added to frames to make cabinet backs or doors. The material you use depends upon the location of the panel. If the panel is used for the cabinet back and will not be visible, you can use hardboard or ¼ inch plywood. However, if the panel in the back will be visible, it might be better to use boards joined together or a decorative hardboard or a hardwood-veneered plywood.

If the panel is used for a door, you can make it out of joined boards, hardwood-veneered plywood, decorative hardboard, or plate glass. Here are but a few of the ways in which panels can be secured to a frame:

A. The panel can be mounted flush with the back, extending to the outer edges of the sides top and bottom. The panel can be fastened with adhesive, nails or screws.

B. The rear pieces can be cut with a rabbet to receive the panel. It is best to cut all the pieces—top, sides and bottom—before they are assembled, although with a router this job can be done after the pieces are securely joined.

C. Easier for a handyman is the use of cleats attached to the inside of the sides, top and bottom. The cleats can be made out of finished molding, ½ inch x ½ inch or larger, or quarter-round molding. The panel fits flush within the opening made by the top, sides and back.

D. The panel can be set in a simple dado or groove cut into the top, sides and bottom edges of the frame. The width of the dado should be the same as the thickness of the panel used.

ADDING LEGS OR A BASE

A finished piece of furniture does not rest directly upon the floor. Either legs of some sort

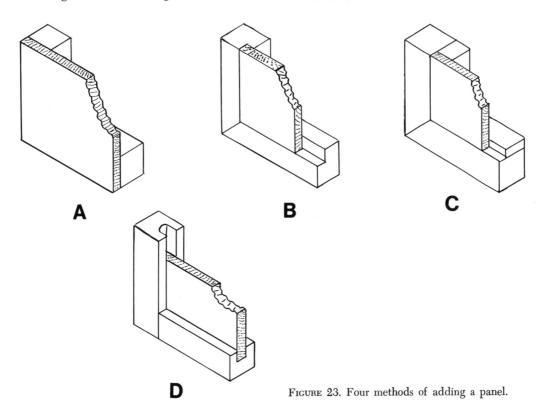

FIGURE 23. Four methods of adding a panel.

are added or a base is anchored to the underside of the unit. Here are several ways in which legs may be added and which are detailed in Section II:

A. A simple butt joint can be used at the corner to join the two rails and the leg. Blind dowels plus adhesive will make a good job. This is the joint most handymen prefer to make because of its simplicity and ease in assembly.

B. A well-fitted open mortise and tenon makes a stronger joint. Tenons are cut on the ends of both rails and the adjoining faces of the leg are mortised to receive the rails. This type joint should be secured with adhesive, plus nails or screws when necessary.

C. The dovetail corner joint is exceptionally strong. It is one of the best methods for the handyman to use. This joint, however, should be cut with power tools. While it is possible to cut the joint by hand, it must be so precise only an experienced woodworker can do the job.

D. A gusset or glue block set in the corner not only joins the two rails but in some cases provides a larger surface to which to attach a leg. This method can be used to make a base; the base is then secured to the underside of the furniture unit by flathead screws driven upward through the gusset.

GLIDES, CASTERS, AND RESTS. Glides are metal, plastic or rubber plates, discs or cushions used under the legs of furniture pieces to protect the floor. They are needed to prevent indentations in resilient flooring materials, scratching, staining and sometimes indentation of wooden floors and the flattening of carpets and rugs.

Casters are wheel or ball-bearing units used to

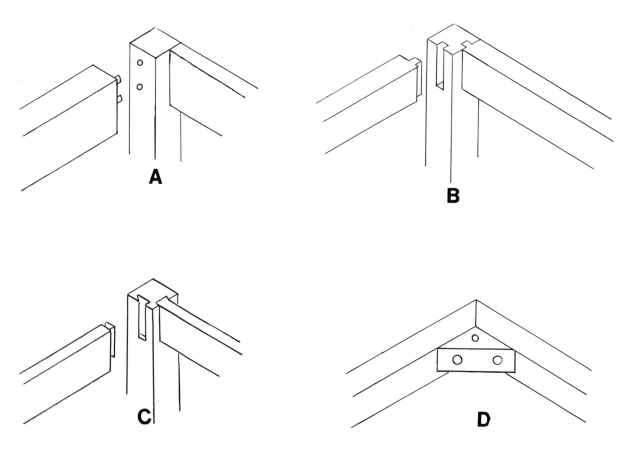

A

B

C

D

FIGURE 24. Four methods of adding legs or a base.

make furniture easily movable. They are attached to the bottom of the leg in place of a glide.

Rests serve the same function as glides but are not attached to the furniture. They are placed under the furniture leg between it and the floor.

HOW TO MAKE DRAWERS

The front end and sides can be put together in several different ways. The four most common cover virtually any type drawer that you would make in the projects described in Section II. Each has certain advantages and limitations.

A. BUTT CORNER—simplest to make but is used where appearance is unimportant; a general all-purpose utility drawer corner.

B. RABBET CORNER—most commonly used about the house; easily made with only a few hand tools; is fairly strong.

C. DADO CORNER—used mostly for small drawers which are not subject to strain or heavy use.

D. DOVETAIL CORNER—strongest of all type corners; used primarily in furniture and fine joinery; comparatively easy to make with hand tools.

ATTACHING THE BOTTOM. When placing the bottom of a drawer in place, it is best to leave some room for shrinking and swelling. This usually is not necessary when either pressed wood or plywood is used. Yet even in these cases, it is best to allow for some freedom of movement.

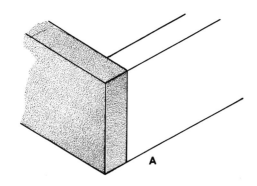
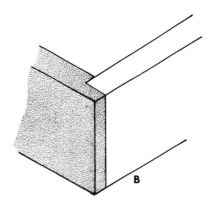
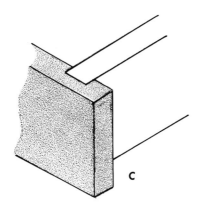
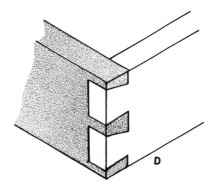

FIGURE 25. Four corner joints used in making drawers.

Therefore, when attaching the bottom to the fronts and sides:

A. Make certain that the grain of the lumber used for the bottom runs parallel to that of the front end.

B. If bottom is held by dado, glue it to front end only.

C. The back end of the drawer should rest on the bottom; or

D. The dado cut in the back end should be wide enough to permit free movement of the bottom if it swells or shrinks.

FIGURE 26. Various methods of attaching a drawer bottom.

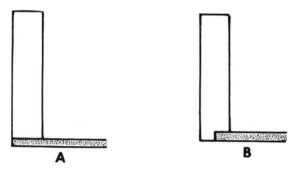

(A) Drawer bottom attached flush with side.

(B) Inserted in rabbet cut in side.

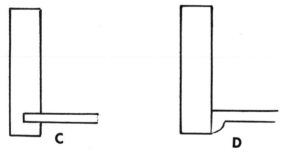

(C) Dado to hold drawer bottom.

(D) Quarter round added to bottom and side.

ADDING A FACE. To make the front end dust-free—that is, the front end cover of the opening provided for the drawer—you can:

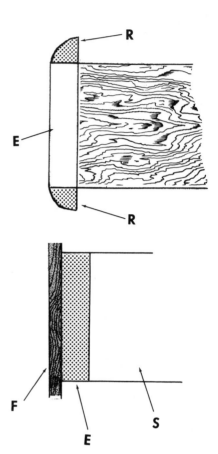

FIGURE 27. Adding a face to a drawer.

ABOVE: Quarter-round (R) cut and mitered to fit around all four sides of front end (E).

BELOW: Decorative face (F) held by screws through front end (E) after sides (S) are attached.

1. Make the front end wider and higher than the side so that it is close up, in fact flush, against the drawer opening frame; or

2. Add 4 pieces of quarter round around all four sides of the front end; these corners should be mitered. The molding should be the same thickness as the front end; or

3. Add an extra-large piece of lumber as a face over the front end. This is often used to conceal homemade dovetail joints. It can also be used when decorative drawer fronts are desired. The face is attached to the front end by screws from

the inside of the drawer, through the front end and into the face. The screws do not come through the face.

HOW TO MAKE DRAWERS SLIDE

Nothing is more annoying than a sticky drawer. Therefore, when you make your own early American furniture make provisions for easy-to-slide drawers. If you have a power saw available you make dado cuts in the drawers or cabinet sides and attach a wood sliding strip. You can also construct the drawer so that slides on a lip are formed by the extended drawer bottom. If power tools are not available, wood strips fastened to the inner face of the cabinet will form a slot for the slide.

Other methods of making a drawer slide are shown in the illustration here and on page 48.

FIGURE 28. Four conventional siding arrangements for drawers.

TOP LEFT. Drawer with dadoed sides can slide on wood strips glued to the sides of cabinet.

TOP RIGHT. An alternative method is to dado the side of the cabinet and glue wood strips to drawer.

BOTTOM LEFT. The drawer can also be made to slide on lip formed by the extended drawer bottom.

BOTTOM RIGHT. If power tools are unavailable wood glued to inner face of cabinet forms slot.

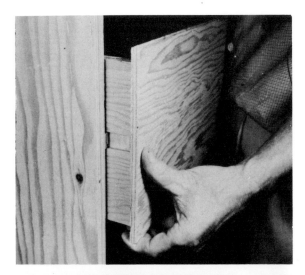

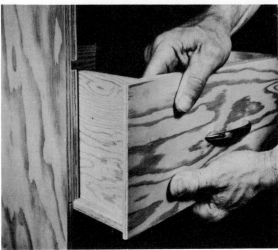

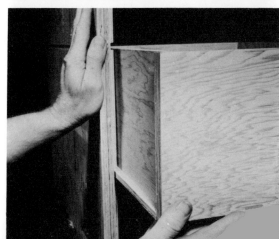

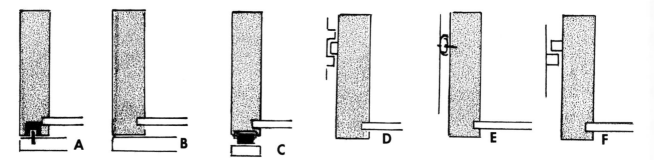

FIGURE 29. Methods of making a drawer slide.

(A) Rubber roller used to move over guide.

(B) Side rests and moves over fixed bottom.

(C) Slide moves over special fiber guide.

(D) Attached side guides hold drawer steady.

(E) Phonograph-type slide holds drawer straight.

(F) Side guides used as roller for drawer.

HOW TO TREAT AN EDGE

Plywood edges can be a problem. If care is not exercised, the finished job will be bonded with raw edges that resemble half-healed scars. First, check the design of the piece to be built. Even with plain butt joints, there are an astonishing number of ways to assemble a simple box, and each one makes a difference in the number of visible edges. By using rabbets and miters, a little thought at the design stage will reduce the edge problem. Consider also where the piece of furniture will be located, what surface will be exposed, and what finish you will use.

Three ways of solving the plywood edge problem are shown on page 49. Of the three, the veneer tape, available in wood grains, can be obtained. It consists of a precut ¾-inch strip of thin wood veneer with its own adhesive applied on the back. After the tape is applied according to manufacturer's instructions, it is finished exactly the same as the panel faces—with stain, varnish, lacquer, paint, or other finishes.

HARDWARE INSTALLATION

The varieties of styles of early American furniture hardware are fairly large, but the installa-tion is rather similar. Here is how to install the major types.

HOW TO HANG SWINGING DOORS. There are several different styles and designs of hinges from which to select when you mount swinging doors on the project described in Section II. Usually, the better hinges come with mounting instructions, some even with templates or patterns to make attaching the doors a simple job. Here are several different ways (illustrations on page 50) in which hinges can be added to swinging doors and cabinets:

A. SIMPLE BUTT HINGE—both the side and the door (shaded section) can be mortised for the hinge, or, if you do not mind the gap, no mortise is necessary. On the left is a view of the door closed; on the right is a view of the door open. Full-mortise, loose-pin, and bullet-tip butt hinges are well designed for modern cabinetwork. Where two dimensions are given for butt hinges, the first always indicates the length of the joint, not including the tips; the second dimension indicates the full width when the hinge is open. The size of a hinge, within certain limitations, has no relation to its weight or strength. The latter depends upon the gauge and kind of metal used.

B. MODIFIED BUTT HINGE—the door (shaded section) is mounted so that it projects slightly in

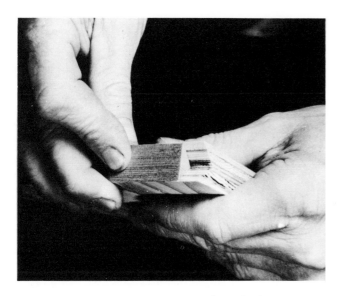

FIGURE 30. Three methods of treating plywood edges.

ABOVE: Matching wood strips may be glued to edge in a "V" groove.

ABOVE RIGHT: A straight strip of wood makes a neat job.

RIGHT: Thin wood banding backed with adhesive is easiest to apply.

front of the edge of the cabinet side. On the left is a closed view of the door; on the right is a view of the door open. Note that the side of the cabinet acts as a door stop.

C. OFFSET HINGE—here the door is rabbet cut and the hinge is recessed in the door next to the cabinet side. On the left is a view of the door in the closed position; on the right is a view of the door (shaded section) in the open position. Note that the door does not open all the way. Although concealed hinges are not entirely invisible, only the edges of their thin joints show when the door is closed. One half of the hinge is set in a grain cut in the top or bottom edge of the door, while the other half is set in the frame.

D. PIVOT HINGE—the hinge is attached to the top and bottom edge of the door (shaded sec-

tion) and the top and base of the cabinet. On the left is a view of the door closed; on the right is a view of the door in an open position. With this type of hinge the door opens all the way.

E. INVISIBLE HINGE—if you do not want any hinge shown, you can use invisible hinges which are set in the edge of the door and frame. They come in a variety of sizes, with the length of the plates ranging from 1 to 5 inches and the width from ⅜ to 1⅜ inches. The mortise is cut out with a router and the hinge attached. On the left is a

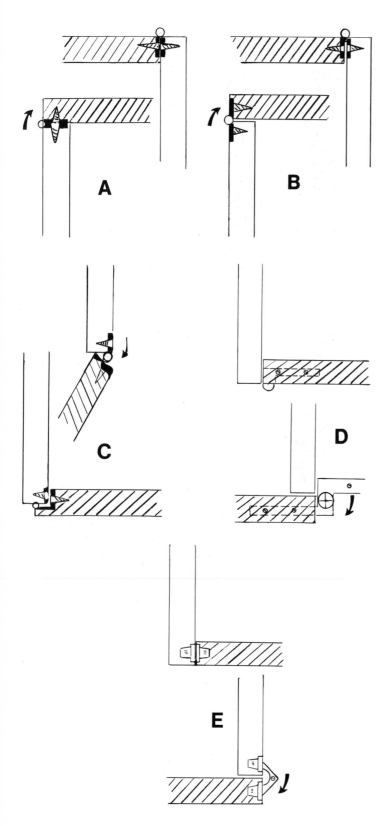

FIGURE 31. The more common hinging arrangements:

(A) Simple butt hinge.

(B) Modified butt hinge.

(C) Offset hinge.

(D) Pivot hinge.

(E) Invisible hinge.

view of the door (shaded section) closed; on the right is a view of the door open all the way.

Drop-leaf hinges are used in good furniture construction for drop leaves of tables and cabinets. The longer half of the hinge must be long enough to reach across the joint and have the screws set in the drop leaf. The center pin is in line with one face of the hinge, so that it may be set without gaining or cutting out for the whole hinge; however, it is necessary to gouge out a groove for the hinge joint. When these hinges are set, the center line of the pin must coincide with the center of the arc which marks the rule joint. The leaves are, of course, first cut with a drop-leaf table cutter on the shaper.

CATCHES. Probably the oldest and most common is the elbow catch, which is screwed to the back of the door. Most catches are spring catches which are released by pulling the door; the elbow catch must be manually released before the door can be opened.

A newer type is the friction catch. Some friction catches are easily applied, being simply screwed in place, while others must be set in holes that are bored for them. Magnetic catches are also available.

Drawer pulls and knobs are never applied to furniture until after the finishing is complete. This makes it easier to do the finishing, since they are not in the way. Without going into the possibilities of metal, or other manufactured pulls, the possibilities with wood alone are vast.

Full wood finishing techniques are covered in Section III.

RUSH SEATS FOR CHAIRS

The chairs in Section II are designed for rush. Real rush or cattail is better than imitation fiber for chairs of good design, although more skill is required to weave it.

The kind of rush used for chair seating is known as cattail. Cattails grow in shallow fresh water, wet swampy places, along the banks of streams, and in lowlands and marshes. They are commonly found in most parts of the northern states. They can be gathered easily and with little or no expense, and, if properly chosen and prepared, are easy to use. Rush also may be bought. Stock ordered from a reliable dealer usually is well cured.

HOW TO COLLECT AND DRY RUSH. You can tell cattails from other plants by their round spikes of flowers—the "bobs" or "cattails." The leaves are in two rows, with their flat sides back to back. There are two kinds: the broad-leafed (about 1 inch wide) and the narrow-leafed. The broad-leafed is more common; the narrow-leafed grows in lowlands and has much longer leaves. Choose the narrow, long leaves (about 7 feet) for chair seating.

Gather the rush when the leaves are full grown, when the stalks are still green, and the tips are beginning to turn brown. Late July, August, or early September is the usual time. Select perfect leaves and those from the stalks that do not have "bobs." Cut the stalks just above the surface of the water or ground. Gather an ample supply. Leaves shrink at least one-third of their weight as they cure; there is waste in weaving as well.

Pull the leaves from the stalks. Sort the leaves, placing together those of about the same width and length, and tie them in loose, flat bundles. Be careful not to bend or break the leaves. Dry them thoroughly for at least two or three weeks in a dark, airy room. An attic or storeroom floor is a good place for drying. Do not put the leaves in a damp room, such as a cellar, where mildew might form on the leaves, or in a hot sunny room where leaves might become brittle.

Rush carefully dried and stored should be usable for a year or more.

GETTING READY TO WEAVE. Smooth any uneven places in the wood and round the edges if they are sharp and likely to break the rush.

Dampen the Rush. Dampen the rush until it is workable enough to twist and weave without cracking or breaking. This may take 1 hour in warm water in a trough, or 8 to 12 hours if spread on the floor and sprinkled.

Fill the trough about three-quarters full of warm water. Add glycerine until the water feels soft, about 1 cup; or use a solution of urea crystals available at drugstores in 1-pound jars, about ¼ cup to 1 gallon of water. Either solution helps prevent the rush from drying out. Glycerine is preferable but costs more. Soak the rush, about a handful at a time, in the solution. You may have to change the solution once before you finish weaving a seat.

You would probably use only water if you dampened the rush on the floor.

Choose and Prepare the Leaves. Choose long, unbroken leaves of about the same length, width, and thickness. The number of leaves to use in each strand depends not only on the leaves but on the size of strand you want. Usually, two leaves are twisted together; sometimes, if they are narrow or thin, three may be used. A thin strand is best for a graceful, delicate chair, but many strands are needed to fill the seat. Thick strands, although fewer would be needed, are too coarse for such a chair. It is important to decide what size strands will look best on your chair.

Select and prepare the leaves and make them into strands as you work. Run the leaves through a wringer to take out air from the cells and to make the leaves workable. Set the rollers tight so that the leaves make a sharp crackling noise as they are run through. Good rush, well prepared, seldom stains the rollers. Draw each leaf quickly over the edge of a metal surface, to take out any air left in the cells.

Practice Making Twists. Cut off about 1 yard

FIGURE 32. How to make the twists.

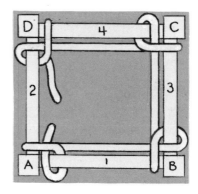

FIGURE 33. By numbering rails with pencil, you can follow the steps without error. A short loop makes the fiber easier to handle in the work.

of cord, and loop it around the back rail of the seat. Tie the ends of cord in a square knot; keep the loop about 5 inches long. Arrange two leaves with a butt end and a tip end together and the flat side of one next to the rounded side of the other, like stacked spoons. Put one end of the pair through the loop of cord for about 3 inches. Fold it toward the front rail and use the ends of string to tie around the bunch, making a square knot near the fold of rush. Tie the string temporarily around the side rail. Twist the leaves together, away from you and in such a way that the strand is smooth, even, tight, and of good color. Usually the thumb and first two fingers of one hand are used to make the twist, and the thumb and fingers of the other hand hold it. Keep the separate leaves straight and smooth as when making a braid; make long but firm twists, with the thumbs about 2 inches apart. Practice until you can make a smooth, even strand that is of a good size for your chair. Then untie the string around the side rail and take out this practice strand before starting to weave.

FIBER RUSH. Fiber rush is made from a very tough grade of paper twisted into a strand to resemble rush. It may be purchased in dark brown, in widths of $\frac{3}{32}$ inch, $\frac{4}{32}$ inch, $\frac{5}{32}$ inch, and $\frac{6}{32}$ inch to resemble antique rush seats, and, in multicolored strands, in a width of $\frac{5}{32}$ inch to resemble new seats.

Buy the fiber in pound or two-pound lots or in quantity on a large reel. That in pound lots costs a few cents more; that in reels takes time and patience to unroll and rewind. Handle that on a reel

as you would wire; that is, roll and unroll it rather than pull it. Take off about 25 yards to work with at one time. Tie the end to a nearby strand, and wind it in a roll about 6 inches across. Twenty-five yards of $\frac{5}{32}$-inch-width fiber weighs about one-half pound. Tie string in a slip knot around the roll so that it will not unwind or untwist.

The techniques of weaving fiber rush and natural rush are similar.

HOW TO WEAVE. The weaving of a firm, smooth seat takes much skill and practice. How you do it depends on the way you like to do it and how you want it to look. One satisfactory method is described in the following paragraphs.

SEATS WITHOUT CORNER BLOCKS. With a carpenter's square as a guide, make a square of stiff cardboard, with the long side about 15 inches. Use this to mark off a square center opening. Place the short side of the cardboard square parallel to either the front or the back rail and the long side against the inner edge of the corner of the back rail. Using a pencil, mark the edge of the square on the front rail. Do the same on the other side of the seat. The two corner measurements may not be the same, but the distance between pencil lines on the front rail must be the same as between posts on the back rail.

Weave the corners first until you reach the

marks on the front rail and then weave as for a square seat. To do this, face the front of the chair and push the loop of string that was used for the practice twist close to the back post on the left side of the seat.

Begin with 4 leaves, each long enough to reach around three sides of the seat. Make 2 pairs, each with a butt and tip end together and the flat side of one leaf next to the round side of the other, as indicated on page 52. Place one end of the pair through the loop of cord for about 3 inches. Fold it toward the front rail and use the end of string to tie around the bunch, making a square knot near the fold of rush.

Choose one pair of leaves, bring them almost to the front rail, and then twist them into a strand. Turn this twist away from the post; keep all other twists in the same direction like a rope. Draw the strand over rail 1, close to post A, up through the opening of the chair, over the side rail 2, again close to the corner post A, and up through the opening again, thus holding the beginning of the twist. Lift up the strand from the underside of the seat to shorten its length and thus help to make the seat firm. Lay the strands in position to make a square crossing and a seam straight from the corner of the seat.

Pull the strand, without twisting the leaves, across the front of the seat. At post B, twist the leaves, bring the strand over side rail 3, close to post B, up through the opening of the seat, over front rail 1, again close to post B. Arrange the strands as at post A.

Pull the strand, without twisting, to the back and fasten it firmly by winding the ends around the back rail and tying them together, or by holding them with a clamp clothespin.

The strands should be twisted only over the rails where they will show, not on the underside of the seat.

Weave the second pair in the same way. Loop the ends tightly around the back rail and fasten them with a clothespin to the first strand. Tie more leaves, one pair at a time, in the same loop of string. About 5 twists fill 1 inch. Use a piece

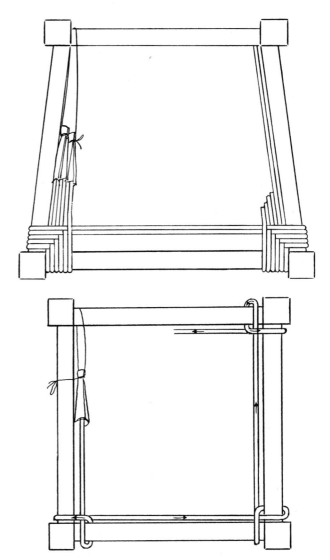

FIGURE 34. Weaving seats without a corner block is shown above, while square weaving can be seen below.

of rush or the cardboard square every 2 or 3 rows to make sure that the corners are square and the rows straight. Use the hammer and block of wood to force the strands in place. Keep the seam straight from the corner toward the center of the seat. Make a square crossing; add from 4 to 6 inches of another leaf, if needed, to fill the space.

After the corners are woven as far as the marks on the front rail, fasten the ends on the right-hand side: tie with a square knot a piece of string about 18 inches long around all the ends of rush. Loop the ends around the back rail and tie another knot. Pull the strands taut and keep the rows straight and close together. Remove the clothespin and cut away the rush over the rail.

If the rush breaks, replace it with another piece.

PAD THE SEAT. After the front corners are filled in, pad them. The padding is put in the pockets on the underside of seat at each side of the corner seams. Butt ends and short lengths of rush are folded the length of the opening and forced in flat bunches from the center toward the corner posts. To do this, turn the chair over. Use a wooden stuffer and poke a bunch of rush into the pocket on the underside of the seat, from the center to the seam. The finished seat should be hard and flat, or slightly rounded, but not over-stuffed. Rush shrinks as it dries, so put in enough padding to make the seat firm but not "fat." Both front corners should be of the same thickness.

As you continue to weave around all four corners, add padding about every 3 inches. Back corners take less padding than do front corners. When you have finished the weaving, add the last padding by poking in bunches parallel to the last strands.

SQUARE SEATS. Seat frames may be square (see page 52) or have corner blocks that make the opening almost square. Weave these seats and seats that are wider at the front, after you have filled the corners, as follows:

Weave the first strand, corner A. Use the same loop that you had for seats wider at the front, or make a similar loop if you are just starting to weave a square seat. Tie in the butt ends of two leaves, one of which is long, and the other short. Twist and weave around post A. Loops of string never have to be cut; weaving covers them.

JOIN THE RUSH. As you leave corner A, add a new leaf. Place between the weaving and the strand, with the butt end hanging down below the underside of the seat for about 6 inches, or the amount of the stiff end of the leaf, and with

the curved side toward you. Twist this new leaf (about twice) with the other two, to hold them together. The butt ends make a seam on the underside of the seat and should hang down rather than be caught in the weaving. That is, always add a new piece of rush after you finish each corner so that when you are ready to weave the next corner the rush will be securely fastened and you will have enough to go around that corner.

ADDING RUSH. Occasionally you may need to use a third piece of rush to fill out the strand, as when crossing twists at the seam. Weave the first strand to corner B. If the strand is too "fat," drop the end of the shortest leaf. This can be cut off or folded in for padding. Twist and weave around corner B. As you leave this corner, again add a new leaf. Then continue to corner C and weave, as shown in the illustration here. Add a new piece of rush, and proceed to and weave around corner D, again adding a piece of rush.

SPLICING. If the rush breaks or you do not have enough to finish weaving the corner, another piece may be spliced in. After you weave the first half of the corner, add a new leaf at the seam with the butt end extending about 6 inches below the seat. Twist the old leaves once around the new to lock it. Then arrange the leaves parallel and twist all three together. If the strand is too thick, pull out the shortest leaf. Continue weaving the second half of the corner. On the underside of the chair these butt ends will stick down, but at an opposite angle from those used for joining, and will be cut off later.

WEAVE THE REST OF THE SEAT. Go on weaving, as for the first strand around post A to posts B, C, and D, until there is only space for two more rows on the side rails. Continue to make the rush workable by running it through the wringer and zipping it with a metal tool. Smooth the twists. Join a new piece of rush after each corner. Pad the seat as you weave. Keep the strands taut, and rows straight, by pounding them with the block of wood, seams straight and the opposite sides of the chair alike. Check as you go along to see that

FIGURE 35. As successive rounds are placed, a pocket is formed between the top and bottom layers. Pack the pocket with wadded brown paper to form a bulge. Tie on new lengths of fiber with a square knot.

the opposite openings measure the same and that you have the same number of twists over each rail. Occasionally force the metal tool quickly between the rows to straighten them and to smooth the strands. Also occasionally, and before the rush dries out, roll and polish the strands with the round end of the stuffer until the seat is smooth.

If the sides are shorter than the back, fill the sides and then weave from back to front in a figure eight: To help prevent holes near the center, weave around the right side rail twice for the last two strands, then proceed to the left rail and weave around it twice. Then weave in a figure eight over the back and front rails until those rails are filled in. Sometimes this process is reversed. Join the rush at the center after weaving the front rail, or after weaving around both rails.

Pull the last few strands through the small opening with a hook made of wire. Weave in as many rows as possible; when you think the seat is filled, add one more strand. Fasten the last strand

on the underside of the chair by separating the ends, winding each one around a nearby strand, and tying them firmly with a square knot.

If the unfinished seat is left overnight, fasten the last twist to the seat with a clamp clothespin. Cover the seat with wet cheesecloth, to keep the rush from drying out.

Techniques for finishing rush seats are given in Section III.

SPLINT SEATS AND BACKS

Splint seats and backs are made of wood that has been cut in long thin strips and interwoven in a pattern. Actually splint is obtained from native ash and hickory and from tropical palm trees. The native splint is cut from selected second-growth timber with straight grain. Ash splints, machine-cut to a uniform width, wear well. Hickory splints often vary slightly in width, giving a pleasing effect. The tropical palm tree from which materials like splints are made grows in the Indian archipelago, China, India, Ceylon, and the Malay peninsula. Without its leaves it is known commercially as rattan. The outer bark, stripped in different widths, is sold as cane; the core, split into round and flat strips of different thicknesses and widths, is called reed. These materials are available from dealers of seat-weaving supplies, mail-order houses, and local stores.

They are all sold either in bunches containing enough for one chair or in quantity lots. Costs per seat are about the same. Real splint makes a better-looking seat than does flat reed, but reed may be easier for beginners to weave.

TO PREPARE TO WEAVE. Pull one of the strands of splint from the looped end of the hank, near where it is tied. As you pull, shake the hank so the splint will not tangle or roughen. Bend the piece between your fingers. The right side is smooth; the wrong side splinters. With the smooth or beveled side out, roll the strand to fit the pan or bowl in which it is to soak. Fasten the ends with a clamp clothespin. Prepare 3 or 4 strands in the same way.

Soak the splint in a solution of glycerine, or of urea crystals. Either helps to shape the splint. The crystals increase its strength, but glycerine is preferred because it helps to retain moisture and keep the splint from drying out and cracking. To hasten the soaking process, use warm water in the solution. Lay the roll in the appropriate container and let it soak until it is soft and pliable—about 30 minutes for splint and about 20 minutes for flat reed, flat oval reed, and binding cane. Each time you remove a roll from the pan, put another one in to soak while you work.

HOW TO WEAVE. Weaving is done in two directions: the first, called *warping*, is the wrapping of the splint around the seat rails. Usually this is done from the back to the front of the chair, or the long way of the opening, so that the second step, called *weaving*, can be done across the open rails, from side to side or the short way of the opening. Both sides of the seat are woven so that they look alike when finished. All splints woven one way on the top of the seat are at right angles to those woven the other way. If the front of the seat is wider than the back, weave the center first and fill in the corners later with short lengths.

WARPING. Mark a center rectangle or square the following way: Using a carpenter's square, cut a cardboard pattern of a size that will fit within the chair rails. Fit this close against one back post, parallel with the back rail. Mark the front corner of the square on the front rail. Repeat on the other side of the seat. Check to see that you have enough space for the width of the splint. If the two sides vary, adjust by marking a slightly greater allowance on the shorter side and less on the long side. On the front rail, mark the center between these two marks. Mark the center on the back rail.

Take the roll of splint from the bowl in which it is soaking and remove the excess water with your fingers, sponge, or cloth. Put another strand in to soak while you work.

Work with the full length of the strand. Tie one end to the left side rail with string, with the right side of the splint next to the wood, so that you are working with the grain. Pull the strand under, and then up and over the back rail, close to the post, in the exact position and shape you want it to dry. Pull the strand to the front rail, with the outside edge exactly at the pencil mark. Pull the strand over and under the rail and then return it to the back rail. Continue until you have used all the strand. Force the wet warpers close together so they will not slip on the rail—strands are apt to shrink more in width than in length—and keep the strands equally taut. Hold the end temporarily with a clamp clothespin.

To join strands on the underside, place a new piece under the old, with the right side down. Lay a stick of soft wood across the rails, under the strands, and staple the strands together in three places, 1 to 2 inches apart, so that at least one of them can be covered when you weave the other way. Pull the strand away from the stick and use pliers to flatten the sharp ends of the staples. Leave enough of the old strand to support the new, but cut off any that would make a double thickness around the rail. Pull the new strand under and around the rail.

Continue warping strands. When you reach the center mark, count the warpers to make sure you will have the same number on each half of the seat. When you reach the pencil mark on the right side of the chair, use a clamp clothespin to hold the warper. If the work is interrupted, sprinkle the seat and dampen the end to keep the splints pliable.

You may wish to use the design shown in Project 5 (page 65) or work out your pattern on squared paper, using one square for each warper. In any case, count the number of warpers on the back rail. This number may be evenly divisible by the number in the design you want to use: for example, 20 strands and a mesh of 2 over 2 under, or 21 strands with a mesh of 3 over and 3 under. If the number is not evenly divisible, you may use the same design if you:

1. Plan from near the center of the opening and begin weaving accordingly. Example: If

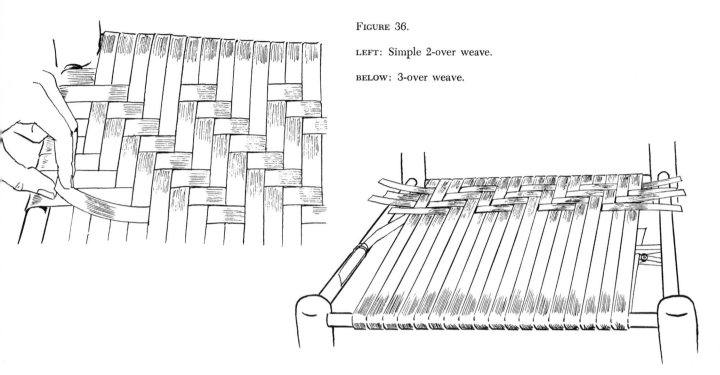

FIGURE 36.

LEFT: Simple 2-over weave.

BELOW: 3-over weave.

there are 23 strands and a mesh of 3 over and 3 under, weave over 1 to start the row, continue across until you have used 21 strands, and then weave the single strand as on the first side.

2. Plan to use a diagonal design. Emphasis then will be away from the side rails, where the design may or may not be completed. A diagonal design also is desirable if the side rails are uneven.

The second row determines how you use the design. You can move one or more strands to the left for a diagonal design from the right back to the left front of the seat, or you may reverse the direction. For a geometric design, weave alternate rows alike.

Weaving which makes the design, frequently is:

Over 2 and under 2

With finer mesh, strands are difficult to push together closely.

Other designs are:

Over 2 and under 3
Over 3 and under 3

Large seats or seats using narrow strands, ⅜ inch or less, may be woven:

Over 4 and under 4
Over 4 and under 2
Over 5 and under 3

The above combinations may be reversed, such as over 2 and under 4. Coarser mesh may be used occasionally if long strands will stay in place and wear satisfactorily.

WEAVING. Be sure the strand of splint is long enough to weave across the top of the seat and to join on the underside. Loosen the last warper over the back rail, remove the clothespin, and bring the warper from the front under and over the back rail and under the preceding warper. Then bring the strand diagonally in front of the back post, under the side rail and turned so the right side is down. Pull all strands tight and then weave across, right to left.

Pull the weaver over the side rail and weave the underside like the top, going over and under the same warpers. When you join strands, staple from either side, if you know the staples will be hidden under warpers. Or you can cover staples with short lengths of splint tucked under nearby strands. Flatten the sharp ends of staples with pliers, as before. Continue weaving, cutting the old strand inside the rail, even if you waste some of it, and forcing the joining in position. You cannot use the warper strand you tucked under until you get nearer the front.

The second row is over 2 and under 3, but one warper to the left of the first row. Or weave to the right if you want the diagonal in the same direction as on the top of the seat. Use a stick or a screwdriver to force the strands together. At the same time pull the strand across the rails so the seat will be firm.

On the underside, plan from near the center of the opening, where the design is established, how to begin the row and so continue the design used on the top. In this way you will weave over and under the same strands as you did on top.

When you have woven far enough to see the design, and have space, cut off a length of splint for a warper in the corner of the seat. Hook about 3 inches over the weaver that will continue the design, near the back of the seat, or just push the strand in rather than hook it over a weaver, if it

fits snugly. Bring this warper to the underside of the seat and hook it over a weaver, if it fits snugly. Bring this warper to the underside of the seat and hook it over a weaver there also. The strands may be joined on top of the seat, under the warpers, to save splint. If the joining is secure, cut off the old strand so two thicknesses do not show. Also cut the string holding the first strand. The weaving will hold this end in place. Add other short lengths in the corners of the seat, as you have room for them. Warpers should also be cut so the ends can be concealed under weavers. One or two staples and the weaving will hold the joining. Use a screwdriver or similar blunt tool to help with the weaving as you get near the front of the seat.

Continue weaving to the front rail. Finish the underside by weaving as far across as you can and tucking the end under a warper. If the back of the chair is to be woven, warp strands the long way (up and down). Weave across from the bottom up so that you can push the strands in place easily. Back warping and weaving are done in a manner similar to that for a seat.

Techniques for finishing splint seats and backs are given in Section III.

SECTION II

EARLY AMERICAN FURNITURE

PROJECTS

PROJECT 1—*EARLY AMERICAN DROP-LEAF TABLE*

Furniture artisans in the newly developing United States were strongly influenced by the styles of the mother country. For example, the graceful, refined lines and slender tapered legs of this table are strongly suggestive of the work of George Hepplewhite, renowned English cabinetmaker. Yet it is far from a Hepplewhite imitation—rather it is a distinctive American style.

The table can be built of white pine. It is important to use seasoned wood, since shrinkage would be especially harmful to the doweled and mortised joints. Dowel and glue pieces of 1x10 together and clamp until dry, then rip to proper width for the top and leaves. You may substitute ¾ inch plywood for these pieces if you prefer. The rule joint where the leaves meet the top can be cut on a radial arm saw with the appropriate shaper heads, or you can have this joint formed at a local millworking shop. Another alternative is to use a butt joint here. Cut the scrollwork on the two end pieces and assemble the frame with glue and wood screws. Taper the legs on two sides only—the outside edges are square. Cut the finger joints in the gate pieces, and round the inside edges of the joints in the two swinging pieces. Mortise the gates into the legs, fastening with glue and dowels. The finger joints are then joined together and secured with dowels. Attach the leg assemblies to the frame with glue and screws. Hinge the leaves to the top and secure to the frame with glue and screws driven at an angle through the inside of the frame into the top.

LIST OF MATERIALS
A. Three pieces, each 33¾"x17½"x¾"
B. Four pieces, each 29½"x⅝"x1⅝"
C. Two pieces, each 30"x6"x¾"
D. Two pieces, each 13½"x6"x¾"
E. Four pieces, each 15"x6"x¾"
¼" dia. dowel sticks

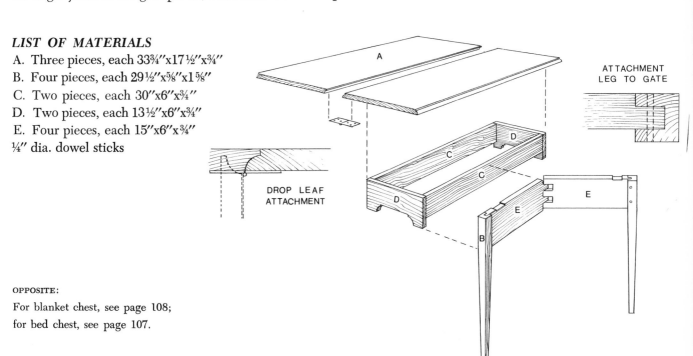

DROP LEAF ATTACHMENT

ATTACHMENT LEG TO GATE

OPPOSITE:

For blanket chest, see page 108;

for bed chest, see page 107.

PROJECT 2—*18th CENTURY CONSOLE TABLE*

The sturdy, simple utilitarianism of this table identifies it as Pennsylvania Dutch in origin, but its graceful proportions and well-turned legs suggest that its creator was influenced and inspired by the work of some of the renowned furniture designers of the late eighteenth century. To reproduce this piece, carefully edge-glue white pine boards together for the top, and clamp until dry (doweling the joints will add considerable strength). Or you may simply use ¾ inch plywood for the top, if you wish. The legs are turned of maple on a lathe—if you do not own this tool, a millworking shop can turn them for you. A ¾x¾ inch frame is attached to the 1x6 pine sides with glue and screws. The sides are then attached to the legs with glue and screws driven through the frame pieces into the legs. This assembly is then fastened to the top, again with glue and screws driven through the frame.

LIST OF MATERIALS

A. Three pieces, each 28″x2½″x2½″
B. Two pieces, each 16″x6″x1″
C. Two pieces, each 34″x6″x1″
D. One piece, 34″x8″x1″
E. Four pieces, each 6″x¾″x¾″
F. Four pieces, each 14½″x¾″x¾″

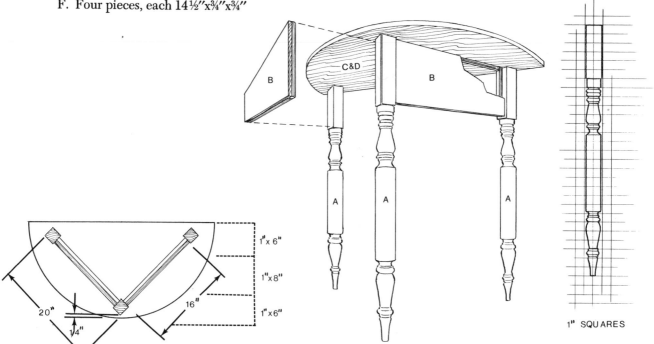

1″ SQUARES

PROJECT 3—
DINING ROOM TABLE

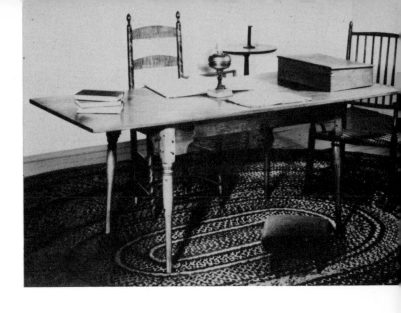

This is a lovely old dining room table that reflects all the charm and simplicity of Shaker construction. The original is made of solid maple with a butternut top but it would be impossible today to find a piece of solid maple or butternut as large (28"x80") as the top of the table. The most practical substitute would be plywood with a cherry or maple facing both for the top and the four pieces of the frame underneath it. The edges of the table top should be concealed with strips of cherry veneer. The legs are turnings and have to be solid. They may be made either from maple or cherry although maple may be much easier to obtain.

Note that the legs have a slight flare. To accomplish this, the rabbeted ends of the side and end pieces (A and B) should be cut at a two-degree angle. In the original the tongues of the side and end pieces are pinned in the leg grooves with ⅜ inch pegs and glued.

Fasten the table top to the frame beneath it with glue blocks, glue and screws. The finish depends on your own taste. Although this piece should be light in color, you will probably have to stain the wood to darken it.

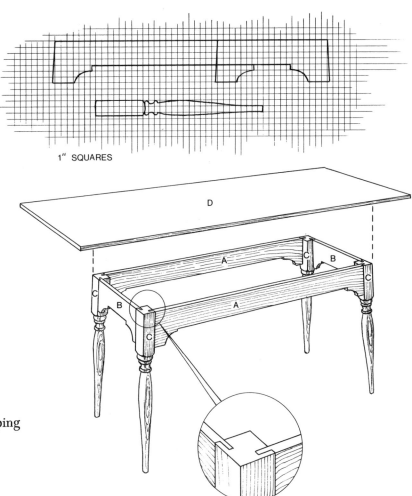

1" SQUARES

LIST OF MATERIALS
A. Two pieces, each 47"x7"x¾"
B. Two pieces, each 19½"x7"x¾"
C. Four pieces, each 29"x2½"x2½"
D. One piece, 80"x28"x¾"
18 feet of cherry or maple veneer stripping

PROJECT 4—*WRITING TABLE*

It is relatively easy to imagine one of the residents of early New England sitting at this table in his library poring over some book or writing in days of yesteryear. It would be equally as easy to imagine yourself or your child sitting at the same table today since it remains as useful as it was then. This writing table reflects all the charm characteristic of colonial furniture with its lightness, sturdiness and simplicity. Because of its simple lines this side table would blend in easily with the most modern decor.

The table top is of the breadboard type which has two separate pieces at the ends to conceal the end grain of the wood. The width of these pieces is not specified but they should not be more than 1½ inches. Use nails and glue to attach them to the single board of the top. If you have difficulty finding a ¾-inch pine board 19½ inches wide, you can glue two narrower pieces edge to edge.

The back (C), sides (B) and two front strips (D and E) are fitted to the legs with glued mortise and tenon joints pinned with ¼ inch dowels. The four triangular wooden braces (G) are notched to fit around the legs (note corner detail) and are fastened with a single screw and glue. Note that the legs are tapered to a ¾ inch square at the bottom. However, the outside edges are straight and only the inner sides of the legs are tapered. Also note that the tapering begins at the bottom of the sides, back and front.

The drawer has butt joints at the back but the sides (J) are fitted to the front (K) with rabbets. Use finishing nails and glue to fasten the drawer together but drive the nails through the sides so that there are no nail holes to mar the front. The drawer runners (I) are ¼ inch thick and protrude only ¼ inch. The drawer groove which rides on these runners should be made to allow 1/16 inch clearance (9/16x5/16) to permit easy movement. Lubricate the runners with paraffin or silicone spray.

The original finish was a clear varnish. If a

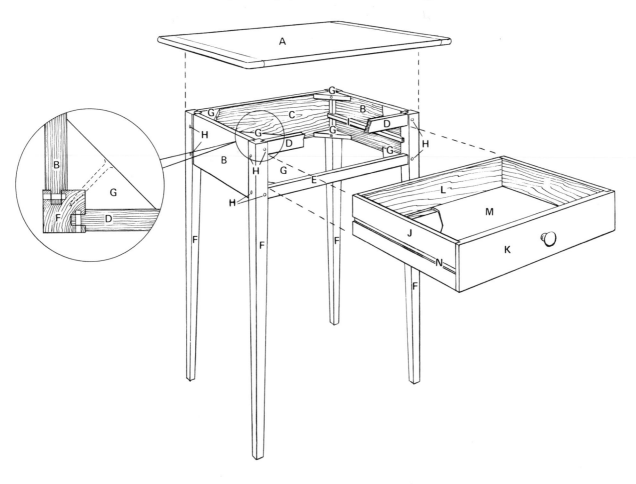

clear finish on a test piece of pine makes it look too white, you can use a light birch stain to impart more "age" to the wood before applying clear lacquer, varnish or penetrating finish or just plain linseed oil.

LIST OF MATERIALS

A. One piece, 24"x19½"x¾"
B. Two pieces, each 5½"x13½"x¾" (including ½" tenons each end)
C. One piece, 5½"x18"x¾" (including ½" tenons each end)
D. One piece, 18"x1¼"x¾" (including ½" tenons each end)
E. One piece, 18"x1"x¾" (including ½" tenons each end)
F. Four pieces, each 27¾"x1½"x1½" taper inside to ¾" square at bottom)
G. Eight pieces, each 4½"x1¾"x¾"
H. Sixteen pieces, each ¼"x1¹³⁄₁₆" dowel.
I. Two pieces, each 13½"x1"x½"
J. Two pieces, each 13½"x3¼"x½"
K. One piece, 17"x3¼"x½"
L. One piece, 16"x3¼"x½"
M. One piece, 13⅛"x16⅜"x¼"
N. Groove, ⁹⁄₁₆" high x ⁵⁄₁₆" deep

PROJECT 5—
STRAIGHT-BACK CHAIR

The chair shown below left is rather simple as far as chair design goes. Over the years, we at *Family Handyman* have not included chair projects in our publication. But in this book, we show several of the simpler ones that *can* be constructed in the home workshop. Remember, however, that chair making is not the easiest of shop tasks.

One and half-inch diameter turned stock is employed for legs, while ½" diameter stock is used as supports. The back pieces are made from ⅜" material. The seat can be woven as described in Section I, page 55.

LIST OF MATERIALS

A. Two pieces, each 50½"x1½" diameter
B. Two pieces, each 19½"x1½" diameter
C. Two pieces, each 16"x½" diameter
D. Six pieces, each 14"x½" diameter
E. Two pieces, each 13½"x½" diameter
F. Three pieces, each 13½"x3½"x⅜"

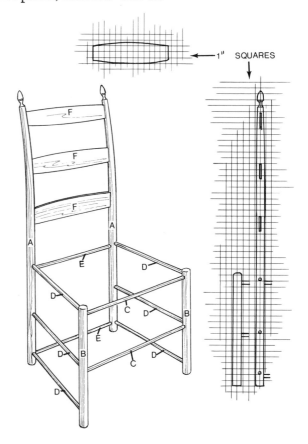

PROJECT 6—
DROP-LEAF TABLE

Many connoisseurs of Shaker furniture consider the pieces made in the community of Hancock, Massachusetts, to be the finest of all. High praise indeed.

This cherry drop-leaf table was built in one of these communities in the early 1800's. As you can see, it is not warped at all, thanks to the air-dried wood used. It can be built easily, following the drawings. We have retained the original method for supporting the leaves when they are up; you can save time using modern hardware—but what you gain in time you lose in authenticity.

To make the support the Shaker way, cut out a long narrow section from the top of the skirt, bevel-cutting the ends as shown, then replace it in the cutout, attaching it with a dowel at the indicated pivot point. With the leaf down, the section fits neatly into the skirt; swing it out when you want the leaf up.

The small dimensions of the table make 1 inch boards, which come trimmed to ¾ inch thick, practicable for construction. You could use ¾ inch plywood, but hiding the exposed plies at the rule joint (where the top meets the leaf) is tricky.

If you do use ply, make all male joint members at least ⅜ inch thick for strength.

LIST OF MATERIALS
A. Two pieces, each 29½"x6"x¾"
B. Four pieces, each 27¼"x1¾"x1¾" tapered
C. Two pieces, each 14¼"x¾"x¾"
D. One piece, 14¼"x6"x¾"
E. One piece, 15¼"x6"x¾"
F. Two pieces, each 4"x2"x¾"
G. Two pieces, each 11"x1½"x¾"
H. One drawer, size to fit, using ¾" face stock
I. One piece, 41"x16¾"x¾"
J. Two pieces, each 41"x9¾"x¾"

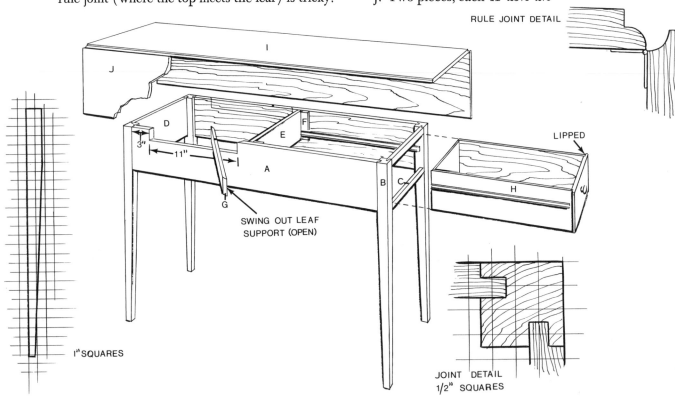

RULE JOINT DETAIL

SWING OUT LEAF
SUPPORT (OPEN)

LIPPED

1"SQUARES

JOINT DETAIL
1/2" SQUARES

PROJECT 7—*UTILITY WORK TABLE*

Whether it is used as a breakfast table in the kitchen, an odds and ends table in the hallway, a game table in the recreation room, or what you will, this early American drop-leaf piece is highly practical, as well as beautiful and sturdy. Originally built in the Shaker community of Sabbathday Lake, New Gloucester, Maine, its two leaves fold down for convenient space saving and fold up to enlarge the work, eating, playing surface.

The table top consists of two leaves (B) attached to a center panel (A) with hinges; it (A) is attached to the frame at the front, back, and side skirts (C, D) with dowels (1), as well as glued to the skirts (C, D), the top of the legs (F), and the corner braces (H)—all to provide a larger bonding surface. The table top overlaps the skirts (D) by 4½ inches.

The skirts (C, D) are slightly recessed in from the legs (F) and are joined by glued mortise and tenon joints as shown in detail 2. The framework is further strengthened with corner braces (H) secured with screws and glue to the legs (F). The legs (F) are turnings that are left square at the top and shaped below.

The table leaves' prop mechanisms are simply 10 inch long strips (E) beveled at both ends

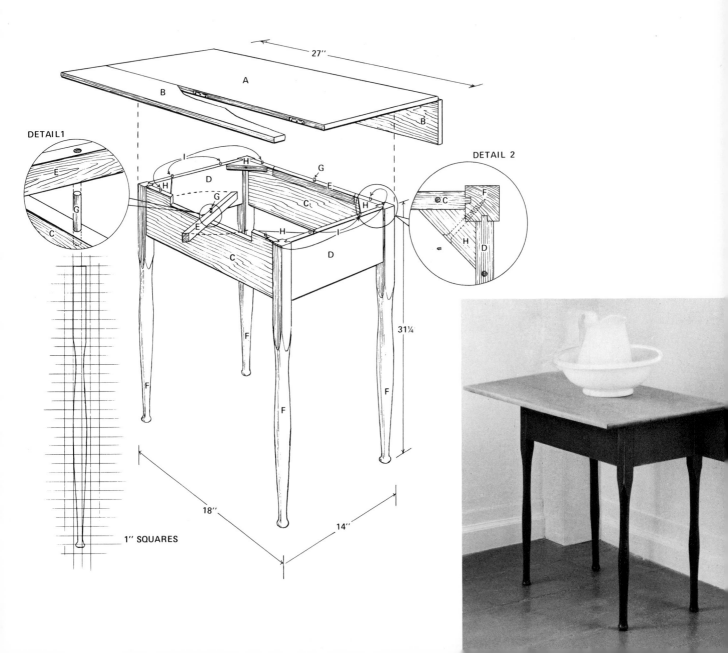

(note that the receiving ends in the front and back skirts (C) must also be beveled) and secured with dowels (G) (detail 1) to allow for rotation.

The original table was made of maple, was stained red, and had a natural top.

LIST OF MATERIALS
A. One piece, 27″x14″x¾″
B. Two pieces, each 27″x6″x¾″

C. Two pieces, each 15½″x5½″x¾″
D. Two pieces, each 11½″x5½″x¾″
E. Two pieces, each 10″x1″x¾″
F. Four pieces, each 31¼″x1½″x1½″
G. Two pieces, each ⅜″ dia. hardwood dowel x 1¾″
H. Four pieces, each 3½″x1½″x¾″
I. Eight pieces, each ⅜″ dia. hardwood dowel x ¾″

PROJECT 8—*SEWING TABLE*

Early American furniture is simple to build, yet sturdy and useful. A piece of furniture that serves beautifully to illustrate these characteristics is this colonial-type table. This table would make an excellent writing desk, a sewing table or simply an extra table for occasional use.

Solid maple and pine stock were used to build this table although you could use any other wood. Most of the construction of the table is obvious, but there are some not-so-obvious construction details that should be pointed out. With the exception of the drawer and the corners of the

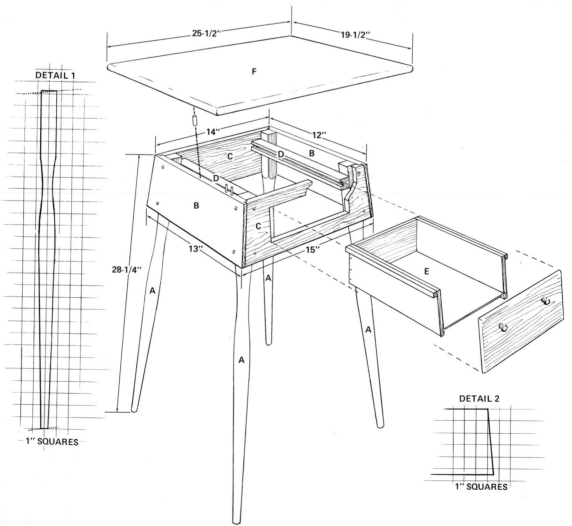

table, butt joints are used. The corners of the table are rabbeted together and the sides, front and back of the drawer are dadoed or grooved to fit over the drawer bottom.

The legs for the table are turned on a lathe using the pattern in detail 1. Since the legs are joined to the table at an angle, their upper and lower ends will have to be cut so that they fit flush under the table top and on the floor. The top itself is joined to the sides using dowels and glue. The sides of the table slope as shown in detail 2. Because both the sides and the legs slope, the backs of the drawer guides (D) have to be planed at an angle to fit flush against the insides of the legs. Although the legs are joined to the sides in the original using screws and glue, you could also use ½ inch pegs or countersunk flathead screws and fill in the holes with plugs.

The finish is optional, but the original stock had a reddish stain.

LIST OF MATERIALS

A. Four pieces, each 29″x1½″x1½″
B. Two pieces, each 13″x5½″x¾″
C. Two pieces, each 13½″x1½″x¾″
D. Two pieces, each 11¼″x1½″x1½″
E. One drawer: one front, 9″x3½″x¾″; two sides, 11¾″x2⅝″x½″; one back, 6½″x2⅝″x½″; one bottom, 11¾″x6½″x¼″
F. One piece, 25½″x19½″x¾″

PROJECT 9—
EARLY AMERICAN ARM CHAIR

The early American child's arm chair illustrated with Project 8 is made of legs that have been turned to 1¼ inch stock. The supports for this chair may be ½ inch diameter dowels, and they are fastened to the legs as described on page 18. The wood splints for the seat and back may be woven as described in Section I.

While the chair illustrated here is for a child's use, the arm technique could be applied to the other straight back chairs described in this book. The front leg stock would have to be increased proportionately.

LIST OF MATERIALS

A. Two pieces, each 30″x1¼″ diameter
B. Two pieces, each 16½″x1¼″ diameter
C. Two pieces, each 11″x2″x1″
D. Six pieces, each 10″x½″ diameter
E. Three pieces, each 12″x½″ diameter
F. Two pieces, each11″x½″ diameter
G. Two pieces, each 11¼″x½″ diameter (bent to proper back curvature)
H. Two pieces, each 2″x1″ diameter (rounded off as illustrated).

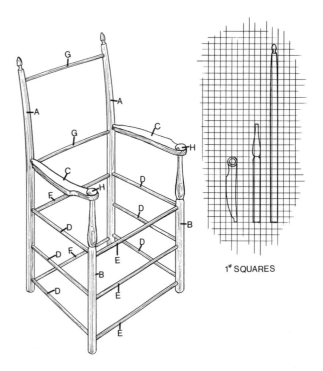

1″ SQUARES

PROJECT 10—*HUTCH TABLE*

Here is the ever popular colonial hutch table, a combination chair and table that is both practical and decorative.

The piece has a circular top 4 feet, 6 inches in diameter, which rests on four sturdy 2x2 inch legs. Drawing No. 1 shows the table assembly with the top raised. Drawing No. 2 is a detail of the arms and their relation to the leg tops. Drawing No. 3 shows the detailed assembly of the table top. Note that while here the top planks are of equal width (six planks, each 9 inches wide), you may use random widths to suit your taste

so long as you keep the total diameter of the top at 4 feet, 6 inches.

Table assembly begins with the leg and seat arrangement. Detail (A) shows the cleats which are attached to the back of pieces (F) and (G). These pieces are set into topped-dado joints as shown, and the cleats attached to the legs, forming the seat frame. Seat slats (C) are plug-screwed to this framework. The term "plug-screwed" refers to a recessed screw covered with a ⅜ inch dowel plug (detail B). The lower rungs are butt-jointed to the legs as shown in detail B. In addition to screws a strong glue should be used on all joints. Screws in rungs and cleats are offset vertically to avoid collision during assembly.

The table top is easily assembled by fastening the planks to the two runners (E) by the plug-screw method. Attach the planks to the runners before cutting the circle. This may be cut with a band saw or keyhole saw. Drawing No. 3 shows table-top assembly. Note the ½ inch hole in each runner for the capped dowel pivot on which the table top swings. Detail C shows rounding principle for table-top edges. As a matter of fact, all edges should be rounded somewhat to give an authentic "colonial" appearance.

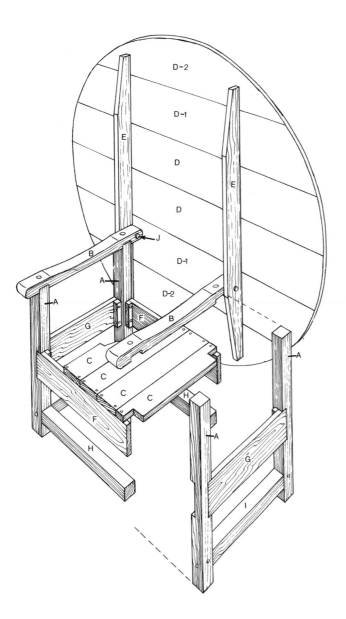

Before attaching the table tops with the pivots, a "clean-up" sanding should be made. Then assemble table top and chair with the capped-dowel arrangement.

LIST OF MATERIALS

A. Four pieces, each 27¾″x2″x2″
B. Two pieces, each 24″x2″x2″
C. Six pieces, each 20″x4″x¾″
D. Two pieces, each 4′6″x9″x¾″
D-1. Two pieces, each 4′4″x9″x¾″
D-2. Two pieces, each 3′6″x9″x¾″
E. Two pieces, each 3′10″x3″x¾″
F. Two pieces, each 20″x4″x¾″
G. Two pieces, each 16″x4″x¾″
H. Two pieces, each 20″x2″x2″
I. Two pieces, each 16″x2″x2″
J. Two pieces, each ½″ dia. dowel x4″

PROJECT 11—
COFFEE TABLE

In colonial days as in modern, the housewife was ever alert for a gadget that would simplify the kitchen chores. The modern housewife in her efficient, fully electric kitchen may view with combined horror and pity the plight of her forebears in the cookrooms of early America. But, considered in proper perspective, things were not so bad for Mrs. Frontiersman, and ingenuity often proved a capable substitute for electrical wizardry in providing culinary conveniences. For example, the old Pennsylvania Dutch kitchen "appliance" shown here made it a simple matter for a lady to pop into the box a few heads of cabbage fresh from her garden, turn on the (muscle) power pushing the box back and forth across the blade and produce the makings of a delicious sauerkraut—a bowl placed below an opening at the blade caught the sliced vegetable. This unusual and clever piece of Americana can easily be reproduced by the modern-day "colonial craftsman"—and it makes a perfect coffee table, with a handy serving compartment for fruit snacks. The plans are for a reproduction faithful in detail to the original, except that we have eliminated the table slot at the slicing blade. We felt that even the most ardent colonial buff would not want to apply the piece to its original usage in preference to a Space Age slaw shredder.

The top piece is of 1¼ inch pine stock. With a dado blade or a sharp chisel, cut a shallow groove diagonally across the top to receive the thin steel "blade"; fasten the steel strip in place with flat-head screws. The legs are turned from 2x2 pine. Drill ½ inch holes in the tops of the legs and in the table, then apply glue and dowel the legs in place, cutting off dowels flush with the table. Use a dado blade to cut grooves the length of the side rails, then fasten these rails to the table with flat-head screws, countersinking and filling the holes with glued-in wood plugs. Assemble the bottomless box and attach glides at each side, then fit into the ⅝ x ⅝ inch grooves.

Finish of thé original slicing table was an antique pine stain, followed by several coats of carefully rubbed paste wax.

LIST OF MATERIALS
A. Four pieces, each 14⅞″x2″x2″
B. Two pieces, each 12″x6″x¾″
C. Two pieces, each 40″x3″x1¼″
D. Two pieces, each 12″x½″x½″
E. One piece, 40″x12″x1¼″
F. Two pieces, each 10½″x6″x¾″
G. Thin steel strip
½″ dia. dowels

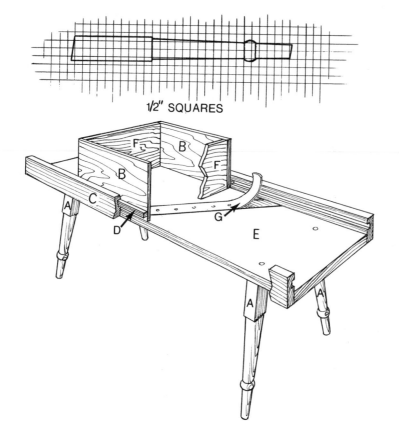

½″ SQUARES

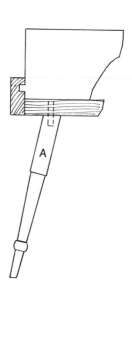

PROJECT 12—
DROP-LEAF END TABLE

For an occasional table with thoroughly early American character, this drop-leaf end table will meet both decorative and functional needs. Folded compactly against the wall with swing-out legs tucked in, usable table surface is a very slim 8 inches by 14 inches—fully expanded, two 12-inch leaves increase the area to a lavish 32-inch spread. There is nothing, however, to prevent you from making a dimensional change here or there to suit your preference, for the design our early craftsman offers allows free modifications at no expense to its appearance.

Cherry would make an ideal stock for this project. Or a clear maple. Even a cabinet pine

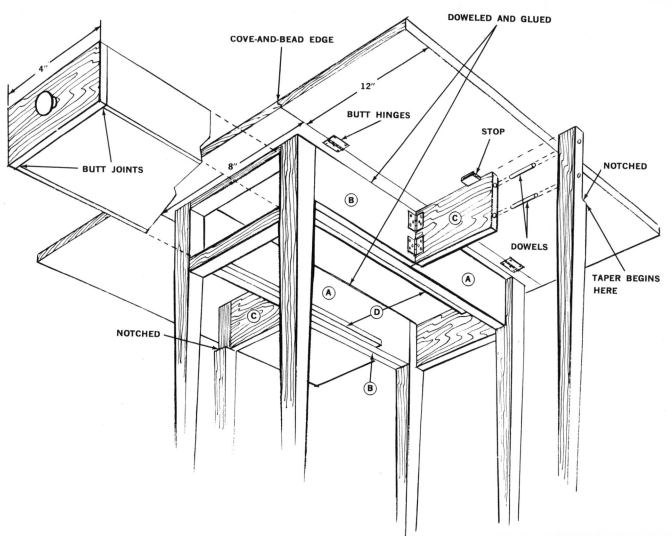

done in a lustrous hard finish with an antique oil. Whatever you select, plan a table height that will serve the exact need; for example, on a level with the couch. And regardless of this height, allow for six legs (1½x1½ dressed) which taper to ⅞-inch, beginning 4 inches from the top (a good guide would be to begin the taper for all six at the notch of the swing-out legs, as suggested by the sketch).

The framing for the table on the long sides may at first seem massive, owing to the construction preferred at the time for accommodating the collapsed leg. Basically, it consists of a full length rail (A in the sketch) joined to the corner legs with dowels, a half-length outer rail (B) and its hinged extension (C), and the drawer rail or support (D). Thus the double-thickness sides (each ¾-inch) fit flush with the leg tops, the drawer supports protruding into the frame's interior, as they should.

The two swing-out legs, as noted, are notched. Simply cut away half the top thickness for a length that equals the width of the full length rail. Joined to the hinged extension of the outer

rail with dowels, the collapsed leg should fit snugly in place—the extension flat against the full length rail with the notched portion of the leg top tucked under. In swing-out position, the extension is halted at 90 degrees by the little wooden stop which is fashioned from scrap.

Having assembled the short, back rail and the two front rails, you can prepare the top. The top is quite hefty: 1⅛-inch stock, the hinged edges routed with the classic cove-and-bead typical of the drop-leaf table. The top is simply glued and nailed to the frame—or you can dowel and edge glue the two long sides and the short end piece.

The drawer is quite small—about 4 inches wide and not too practical for storage other than odds and ends. Butt joints only are used, and the height and width is a good ¹⁄₁₆-inch less, all around, assuring free movement in the opening. Of course, make the drawer only after the frame is assembled.

Because there is some leeway in dimensions and since stock lumber sizes are given in the text, no list of materials is included with this project.

PROJECT 13—*SERVING TABLE*

Owing to its height of 36¼ inches and the emphasis on straight line design, the piece shown here is decidely a server in the Sheraton tradition, an American reproduction with an origin probably in Connecticut, c. 1800. Done in a richly mellow tiger maple, a stock no longer available, your workshop version, shortened to 29 or 30 inches, could easily pass as a dressing table or lady's desk—and would look just as stunning in cherry, ash or something like fiddle-back maple.

Working with solid wood boards, get started first on the top, doweling and edge-gluing, followed by clamping. Going on to the frame, you will see that it makes use of 8 right-angle metal braces, positioned horizontally, each brace joining three parts—upper or lower strut, leg top, and side. Before you can assemble any part of this frame, however, you will have to turn the legs on a wood lathe. The inch-square graph shows the line to follow, using 2x2 dressed stock.

With the legs finished and the 2 sides and 4 struts cut, it is suggested you assemble as follows: Place a leg, a side and a leg on a flat surface, glue the ends of the sides and assemble the three parts with the braces, having first predrilled for the screws. Repeat the process for the other 2 legs and side. For convenience, install the single drawer rail on the inside of each assembly at this time.

Now attach the 4 struts (1x2x30), steadying the end assemblies with scrap stock until you have driven the screws home. Use glue on the ends, as before. All that remains to be attached

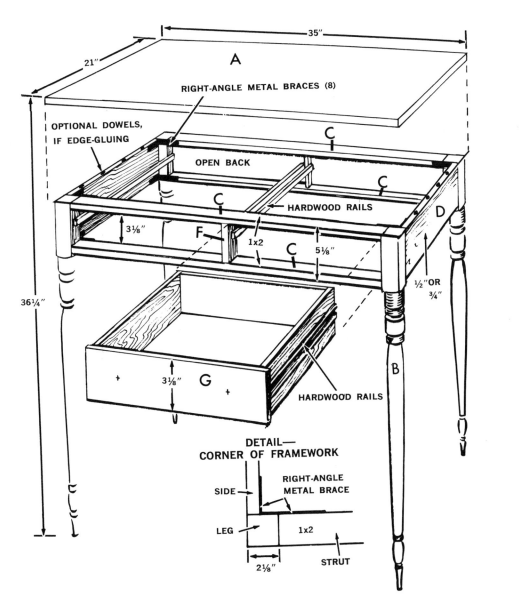

35"

21"

A

RIGHT-ANGLE METAL BRACES (8)

OPTIONAL DOWELS,
IF EDGE-GLUING

C

OPEN BACK

C

HARDWOOD RAILS

D

C

3⅛"

F

1x2

C

5⅛"

½"OR
¾"

36¼"

G

3⅛"

HARDWOOD RAILS

B

DETAIL—
CORNER OF FRAMEWORK

SIDE

RIGHT-ANGLE
METAL BRACE

LEG

1x2

STRUT

2⅛"

1-INCH
SQUARES

are the two short vertical struts and the two remaining single rails.

Getting back to the top, dowel and edge-glue it to the ends, and screw through the struts, into the underside, at the front and back. Or, you can skip all this and screw through the top, into the frame, countersinking the heads, plugging with grain from scrap of the same type. But if you are veneering an old table top or a new plywood sheet, naturally you don't have to be so elaborate about it.

Make two drawers of ½ and ¼ inch stock, using butt joints, glue and nails—and add two double rails to each side for a total of 8.

LIST OF MATERIALS

A. One piece, 35″x21″x1″
B. Four pieces, each 35¼″x2″x2″
C. Four Pieces, each 31″x2″x1″
D. Two pieces, each 17″x5⅛″x¾″ or ½″
E. Twelve pieces, each 17″x½″x½″ (not shown)
F. Two pieces, each 3⅛″x2″x1″
G. Two drawers, each: one front, 15″x3⅛″x¾″; two sides, 19″x2¾″x½″; one back, 14½″x2¾″x ½″; one bottom, 14½″x19″x1¾″

8 right-angle metal braces

PROJECT 14—*HARVEST TABLE*

There is nothing unusual in the construction of the harvest table, a beautiful colonial piece that is equally useful and appropriate in the twentieth century. The top and frame are of 1-inch stock. Boards are doweled and edge-glued together to make the 24-inch top width and the 16-inch width of the leaves, or plywood may be employed. Construct the frame, gluing and nailing together and gluing diagonal corner braces in place. Cut out for the leaf supports, and attach these supports with dowels. The legs are turned on a lathe, then glued to the corners of the frame and secured by lag screws set through the corner braces. Butt joints are used between top and leaves; leaves are fastened to the top with strap hinges, then the top is glued in place on the frame.

LIST OF MATERIALS

A. One piece, 72″x24″x¾″
B. Two pieces, each 72″x16″x¾″
C. Four pieces, each 29″x3″x3″
D. Two pieces, each 48″x5″x¾″
E. Two pieces, each 16½″x5″x¾″
F. Four pieces, each 11½″x5″x¾″ (beveled and cut to fit)
G. Two pieces, each 20″x2″x¾″
Four strap hinges
⅜″ diameter dowels as needed.

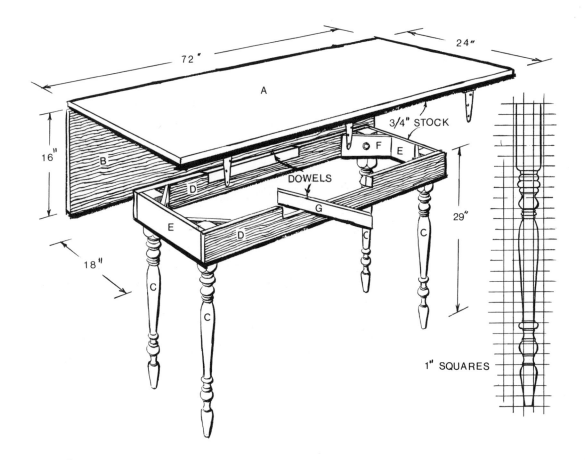

72"

24"

A

3/4" STOCK

16"

B

F

E

D

DOWELS

E

D

G

29"

18"

C

C

C

C

C

1" SQUARES

PROJECT 15—*SHAKER SEWING TABLE*

In the Sabbathday Lake Shaker community in New Gloucester, Maine, this combined chest of drawers and sewing table has the simplicity and functional utility characteristic of Shaker furniture.

The table top is made up of three random width solid planks glued together at the edges to form a 20 inch width and is nailed and glued to the frame beneath it. The framework is made up of 1x2's (B-C-D-E) which are joined to the legs (A) with shallow mortise and tenon joints as shown in detail 1. An alternate method of joining the horizontals (B) to the legs is shown in detail 2 using two 1 inch right-angle braces with screws and glue. The ⅛ inch pegs (R) are used to pin the mortise and tenon joints as shown in detail 3. The verticals (D-E) of the front frame are joined to the horizontals (B) with mortise and tenon joints but the mortises are simply open notches in the backs of the horizontals. Note, however, that the joint where D joins the center rail (B) is a half lap.

The back (M) and sides (L) are covered with ¼ inch plywood from the inside and fastened to the frame with nails and glue. Since these plywood sheets (L-M) do not overlap the legs but only butt against them, half inch quarter round strips (Q) fastened with brads and glue are used to anchor the plywood to the legs. The back is constructed like the sides with three horizontal rails like (B). There are four triangular wooden braces (K) in each corner at the top which are fastened to the rails (C-B) with long screws and glue. To fit around the corner of each leg, these braces have a notch.

The drawer guides (F) are simply half inch strips which would be waxed for easy operation. The verticals (G) in the back are there to support the ends of drawer guides.

The finish on the original was a dark red stain

on the top, sides, back and drawer fronts. The three front rails (B) and fronts of the legs have a clear natural finish.

LIST OF MATERIALS

A. Four pieces, each 31¼″x2″x2″ (see patterns)

B. Five pieces, each 46½″x2″x1″ (including tenons)

C. Six pieces, each 16″x2″x1″ (including tenons)

D. One piece, 13¾″x2″x1″ (including tenons)

E. Two pieces, each 5⅞″x2″x1″ (including tenons)

F. Thirty-six pieces, each 17″x½″x½″

G. Three pieces, each 17¼″x2″x1″

H. One piece, 20″x56½″x¾″

K. Four pieces, each 4″x4″x2″

L. Two pieces, each 15″x17½″x¼″

M. One piece, 46½″x17½″x¼″

N. Four pieces, each 10¾″x5⅜″x¾″

O. Two pieces, each 22½″x8⅜″x¾″

P. Eight pieces, each 4⅞″x16″x½″

Q. Six pieces, each ¼ round 15½″x½″

R. Twenty-two pieces, each 1″x⅛″ dia. dowel.

S. Four pieces, each 8½″x4⅞″x½″

T. Two pieces, each 20½″x7⅞″x½″

U. Four pieces, each 16″x7⅞″x½″

V. Four pieces, each 9¼″x16″x⅛″

W. Two pieces, each 21¼″x16″x⅛″

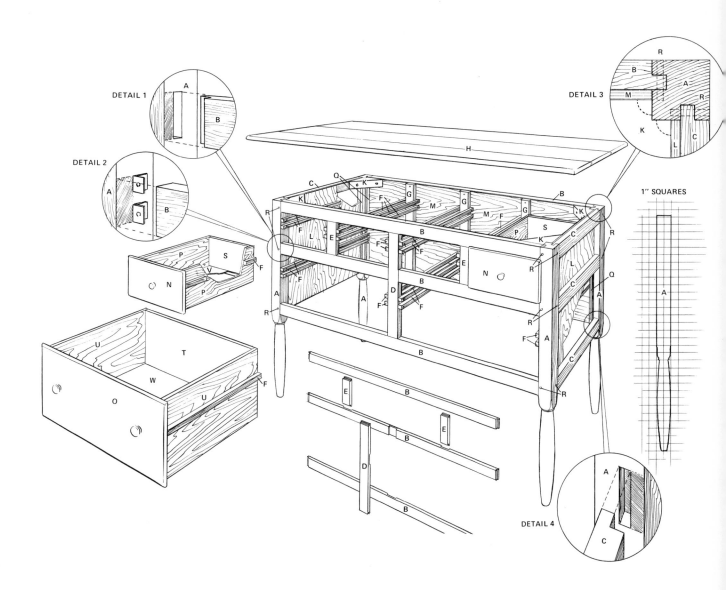

PROJECT 16—DESK AND WORK TABLE

This handsomely designed piece of furniture is billed as a desk and work table. It is that and more, too. With its thirteen drawers and the top section's middle area (with door), it is also a bureau piece that provides abundant space for storage. In addition, the top of the six small drawers section (G) offers a mantel-like area for placing objects, while the good-sized counter (J) and the large pull-out section (K) are available for use as a desk, work table, or drawing board. This Shaker item will fit handily into a corner so that both front and side sets of drawers are easily accessible.

The basic frame of the piece is constructed of

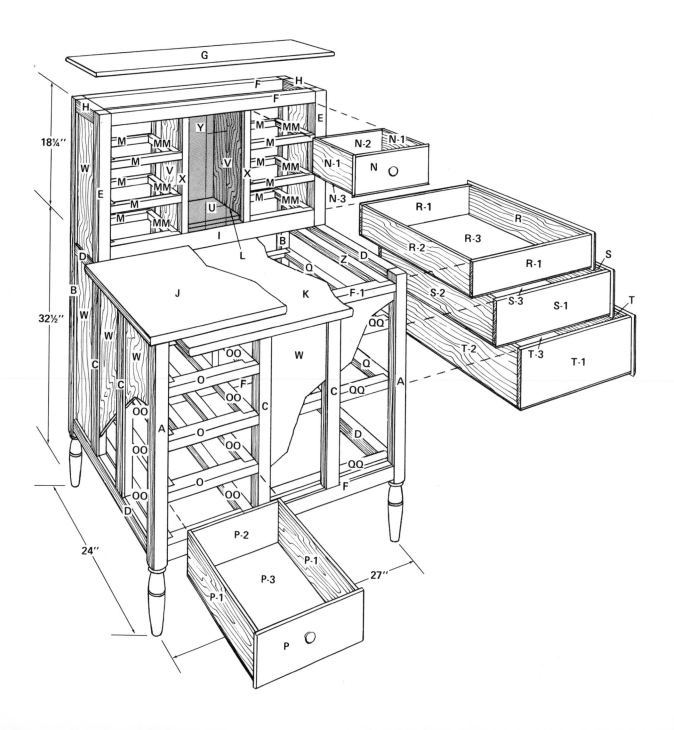

which are attached under the sides, backs, and fronts of the drawers with nails and glue. The four equal-size drawers of the bottom section, when pushed all the way in, reach approximately two-thirds of the full depth of the bottom section; otherwise, the drawers would be much too unwieldy.

The counter (J) can be made from one sheet of plywood, but it is best not to use plywood because the edges will clearly show its layers. It would be best to use two pieces of hardwood (the original was made of maple) edge-glued together and rounded off at the outer edges. The top piece (G) is simply glued to the frame (F,H).

The floor (U) of the middle area between the two sets of drawers in the top section also provides a stop for the flush door (L). The door is joined together with mortise and tenons and has a recessed panel. Finally, the legs of the desk are turnings shaped as shown in the accompanying photo.

varying lengths of 1½x1½'s (A,B,D,E,F,H,) attached with mortise and tenon joints glued together. The front, bottom crossbar of the top section (I) is 1½x2¼, however, to allow ¾ inch as a backstop for the counter (J). The verticals (C) for the panels were originally attached to the horizontals (D,F) with mortise and tenon joints and pegged. If, however, you find this too difficult, you can half lap the verticals to the horizontals and show externally the same results. If you don't want to bother with pegs, you can use countersunk screws with a plug in the top cavity to conceal the screw. In addition, the verticals (C) are recessed in the back 1⅛ inches to allow insertion of ¼ inch panels, leaving a ⅜ inch recess in front.

The members of each of the rectangular drawer guides (M,O,Q) are rabbeted together, with the front members flush with the rest of the basic frame to form the exterior areas between the drawers. The six small drawers (N) of the top section, when pushed all the way in, reach the back panel of the section and have bottoms which are simply glued directly to the sides, backs and fronts of the drawers. The seven drawers of the bottom section have bottoms

LIST OF MATERIALS

A. Two pieces, each 32½"x1½"x1½"
B. Two pieces, each 50¾"x1½"x1½"
C. Six pieces, each 21½"x1½"x1½"
D. Four pieces, each 21"x1½"x1½"
E. Two pieces, each 18½"x1½"x1½"
F. Four pieces, each 24"x1½"x1½"
F-1. One piece, 24"x1½"x¾"
G. One piece, 8½"x28"x⅜"
H. Two pieces, each 5"x1½"x1½"
I. One piece, 24"x2¼"x1½"
J. One piece, 18"x30"x¾"
K. One piece, 23"x24"x¾"
L. Door, 6"x15⅝"x¾"
M. Ten pieces, each 8"x1"x1"
MM. Twelve pieces, each 5½"x1"x1"
N. Six pieces, each 8½"x4¹³⁄₁₆"x¾"
N-1. Twelve pieces, each 7½"x4"x½"
N-2. Six pieces, each 6⅞"x4"x½"
N-3. Six pieces, each 6⅞"x7½"x³⁄₁₆"
O. Six pieces, each 9"x1½"x1"
OO. Eight pieces, each 22½"x1½"x1"

(continued on page 82)

P. Four pieces, each 9½″x5⅛″x¾″
P-1. Eight pieces, each 15″x4½″x½″
P-2. Four pieces, each 7⅞″x4½″x½″
P-3. Four pieces, each 15″x8¼″x3⁄16″
Q. Four pieces, each 21″x1½″x1″
QQ. Six pieces, each 16½″x1½″x1″
R. One piece, 21½″x4″x¾″
R-1. Two pieces, each 15″x3⅜″x½″
R-2. One piece, 19⅞″x3⅜″x½″
R-3. One piece, 15″x20¼″x3⁄16″
S. One piece, 21½″x6½″x¾″
S-1. Two pieces, each 15″x5⅞″x½″
S-2. One piece, 19⅞″x5⅞″x½″
S-3. One piece, 15″x20¼″x3⁄16″
T. One piece, 21½″x9½″x¾″
T-1. Two pieces, each 15″x8⅞″x½″
T-2. One piece, 19⅞″x8⅞″x½″
T-3. One piece, 15″x20¼″x3⁄16″
U. One piece, 5¾″x6″x⅜″
V. Two pieces, each 5¾″x15⅜″x⅜″
W. ¼″ plywood panels to fit
X. Two pieces, each 15⅛″x1″x1″
Y. One piece, 8″x15⅛″x¼″
Z. Slide guides, 21″x1″x1″

PROJECT 17—
DUTCH SETTLE

The Dutch settle is a piece often found in pairs beside a fireplace where the tall back helped shield the sitter from ever-present drafts.

The length of the settle illustrated is optional; it may be built to fit into a specific area of your home. The scrolled sides are each made of 1x12's ripped to a combined width of 22¼ inches. Cut all pieces to size, then assemble the back and sides, gluing all joints, doweling the boards together, and screwing cleats and stiffeners in place. Attach the bottom (1x10's or plywood) to sides and back, then attach the front. Glue and dowel two 1x10's together for the seat, then screw 1x4 cleats to the bottom of the 1x10's using 1¼ inch flathead screws. Fasten the seat to the frame with butt hinges.

LIST OF MATERIALS

A. Two pieces, each 40″x22″x1″
B. Three pieces, each 40″x4″x1″
C. Three pieces, each optionalx2″x1″
D. One piece, optionalx20″x1″

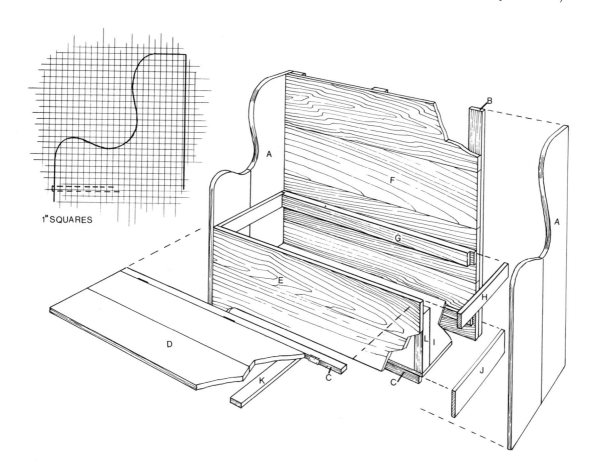

1" SQUARES

E. One piece, optionalx17"1"
F. Three pieces, each optionalx10"x1"
G. One piece, optionalx4"x2"
H. Two pieces, each 19"x4"x1"

I. One piece, optionalx19"x1"
J. Two pieces, each 19"x6"x1"
K. Two pieces, each 18¼"x4"x1"
L. Two pieces, each 7"x4"x2"

PROJECT 18—*COBBLER'S WORKBENCH*

The itinerant cobblers of colonial and frontier times favored the familiar, easily transported straddle-type workbench, of which so many fine examples have survived to the present. With the gradual urbanization of parts of the country, these wandering craftsmen set up shop in their homes or in small stores. More permanent equip-ment was in order, and many cobblers became do-it-yourselfers to outfit their shops. A most unusual product of this era is a workbench built by a Pennsylvania shoemaker in the early nine-teenth century. The name of this cobbler is lost in history, but something of the man can be told from his workbench. He was probably neat

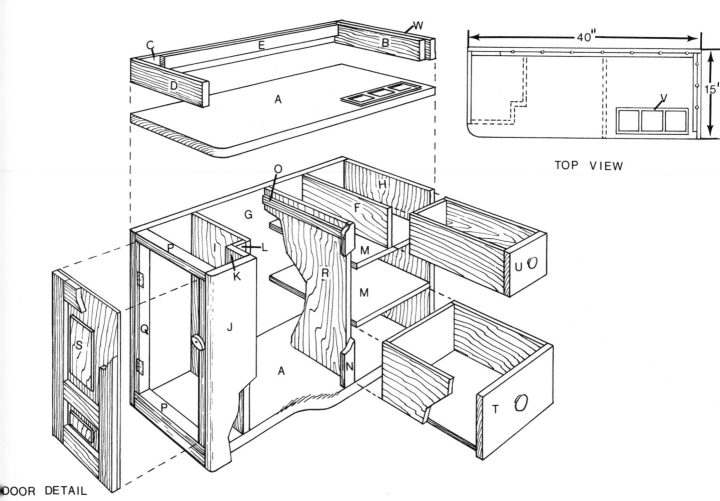

W

C
E
B

D

A

40"

15"

V

TOP VIEW

O

H

G

F

P

I

L

M

K

Q

J

R

M

A

N

S

U O

T O

DOOR DETAIL

and tidy and a stickler for efficient production, since he provided plenty of storage space for tools and materials in drawers, a cabinet, and a toolrack around the edge of the bench top. And he presumably had a somewhat nervous habit of shuffling his feet—a habit that eventually wore down the front edge of the bench floor. We may also attribute a bit of eccentricity or perhaps whimsy to our friend, for certain design details are unusual or even baffling by our standards—such as the jog on the left-end cabinet, or the lonely strip of wood fastened inside the kneehole, or the chunk of log used as a base for the interchangeable shoe lasts, a unique idea at the very least. So we present this piece to you, in its modern role as an escritoire. Our plans show it just the way it was originally built—including the mysterious features—eliminating only the log, which you may choose to place on top or leave off to allow more usable space.

The floor and top of the workbench are of 1¼ inch pine. If your lumber dealer is unable to supply this in 15 inch width, you can edge-glue two boards together, doweling for extra strength if you wish. Plywood may also be used; two pieces can be laminated together to obtain the proper thickness. The back, end, partitions, and dividers are of ¾ inch pine, or again you may use plywood. Cut the floor to shape, feathering the edge at the kneehole. Fasten the partitions to the floor, gluing and nailing through the bottom, then fasten the end piece to the floor and attach the drawer dividers. Glue and nail the back boards to the partitions. Fasten the front panel and build the frame for the door. Now set the top in place, again gluing and fastening with 6d finishing nails. Assemble the toolrack frame around the top, boring holes between the boards to hold awls, knives, and the like. Build the drawers of ¾ inch pine and attach wood pulls with screws through drawer fronts from inside. A drawer lock may be installed on the left-hand small drawer, as in the original. Door panels are glued to the ¼ inch plywood backing and the wood pull is fastened. The door is hung on butt hinges; you may use small cabinet butts, or the true purist may obtain antique hinges from a specialty shop. A wood latch holds the door shut.

You may wish to duplicate the many characteristic nicks, scratches, and gouges that are borne by the original workbench as a result of its long years of faithful service. Edges and corners should be rounded and sanded smooth. Make sure that all nails are set below the surface and the holes filled with wood putty. When final sanding is completed, apply the desired finishing coats.

LIST OF MATERIALS

A. Two pieces, each 40″x15″x1¼″
B. One piece, 13″x2½″x¾″
C. One piece, 40″x2½″x¾″
D. One piece, 12⅛″x2½″x¾″
E. One piece, 33″x1¼″x¾″
F. One piece, 14¼″x5″x¾″
G. One piece, 40″x22¼″x¾″
H. One piece, 14¼″x22¼″x¾″
I. One piece, 9⅛″x21″x¾″
J. One piece, 4¼″x22¼″x1¼″
K. One piece, 2½″x21″x¾″
L. One piece, 1½″x21″x¾″
M. Two pieces, each 14½″x15¼″x¾″
N. One piece, 1½″x21″x¾″
O. One piece, 13½″x1¼″x½″
P. Two pieces, each 9⅜″x1½″x¾″
Q. Two pieces, each 17⅞″x1½″x¾″
R. One piece, 13½″x21″x¾″
S. One door: backing, one piece, 9⅜″x19⅜″x¼″ plywood; frame, two pieces, 19⅜″x2″x¾″; frame, two pieces, 5⅜″x2″x¾″; panel, one piece, 7⅞″x4⅛″x¼″; panel, one piece, 1½″x 4⅛″x¼″
T. Two drawers, each: front, one piece, 15⅛″x 7⅛″x¾″; sides, two pieces, 13½″x7⅛″x¾″; bottom, one piece, 12¾″x12⅞″x¾″; back, one piece, 13⅝″x7⅛″x¾″
U. Two drawers, each: front, one piece, 7⅛″x5″x ¾″; sides, two pieces, 13½″x5″x¾″; back, one piece, 5⅝″x5″x¾″; bottom, one piece, 12¾″x 5⅝″x¾″
V. ½″x½″ pine trim for brad boxes as needed
W. One piece, 14¼″x2½″x¾″

PROJECT 19—*SAILMAKER'S BENCH*

Back in the days when iron men sailed wooden ships powered by billowing sails, the ancient and honorable craft of sailmaking was widely practiced. In the same way that a special type of bench was a work table for a cobbler, the sailmaker had his unique table, too. Like the cobbler's bench, it was instrumental in allowing him to do a better job as he worked away. The table provided not only a work surface but, in addition, a place for him to sit while holding the work on his lap.

Like many another utility piece that had its origins in the workshops of colonial America, the sailmaker's bench is at home today in the living room where it has made a place for itself as a piece of furniture. Its convenient size and height makes it just right for use as a coffee table.

The materials used in the construction of the bench will depend, to a large extent, on their availability. In particular, this applies to the 1x16 pine boards that are used for the top and legs. Stock of this width will not be found at every lumberyard, but many dealers will be able to obtain it for you. As an alternate choice, ¾ inch

pine plywood can be used instead. The remaining materials are readily available.

Following the dimensions in the sketch, cut the top to size, and shape the 1x5 boards on the edge to the contour shown, using a sabre or coping saw. Fasten the 1x5's to the top with finishing nails and glue. Additional nails, driven through the overhanging 1x5's into the sides of the legs, will provide a good degree of rigidity. Attach the few boards that make up the frame of the drawer. Cut and fit the braces between the legs.

Now, only finishing touches remain. Trim the top with ¾x¾ inch stock, as seen in the drawing, and drill a 5 inch hole in the top using a circle-cutting bit in a power drill. A keyhole or sabre saw will also do the job, but the bit is easier to use.

Across the end of the top is a length of 2x4, in which have been drilled five equally spaced ¾ inch holes. The workman used this piece as a tool rack, keeping his unused tools handy by placing them in the holes. After drilling these holes, attach the board to the top with glue and screws. Make the drawer, following the sketch, to complete the piece.

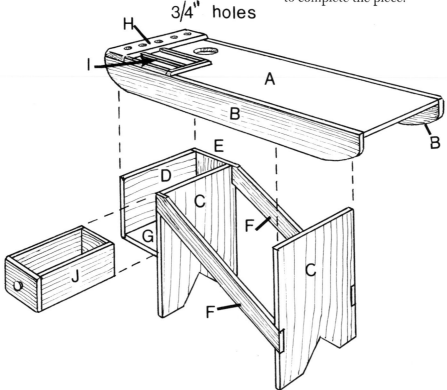

LIST OF MATERIALS

A. One piece, 48"x16"x1"
B. Two pieces, each 48"x5"x1"
C. Two pieces, each 24"x16"x1"
D. One piece, 12"x16"x1"
E. One piece, 8"x12"x1"
F. Two pieces, each 30"x4"x1"
G. One piece, 8"x15"x1"
H. One piece, 16"x4"x2"
I. Four pieces, each 8"x¾"x¾"
J. One drawer: front, one piece, 8"x7"x1"; sides, two pieces, 15"x7"x1"; back, one piece, 6"x 7"x1"; bottom, one piece, 14"x6"x1"

PROJECT 20—*PEG-LEG FOOTSTOOL*

For solid comfort, there is nothing to beat a solid footstool and a favorite chair. Here is one that can be made in a few minutes from a 13 inch piece of 2x10 stock and four 7½ inch pieces of 2x2. The legs may be tapered to suit with a plane; exact dimensions don't matter. Drill 1 inch holes in the top of each leg, making them 1 inch deep. Drill matching 1 inch holes in the top piece and glue the legs in place with length of dowel about 3 inches long. Cut off whatever excess dowel protrudes above the top and sand down flush. Round the edges with a wood rasp to achieve a rough-hewn look.

LIST OF MATERIALS

A. One piece, 13"x10"x2"
B. Four pieces, each 7½"x2"x2"

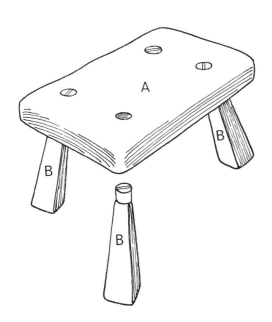

PROJECT 21—CRACKER BARREL

Old-timers still reminisce fondly about gathering at the general store around the old potbellied stove on a cold winter's day, discussing politics, crops, the weather and the townspeople, dipping into the cracker barrel occasionally and munching a crisp cracker or two with a slab of "store" cheese.

That was not so long ago—and the cracker barrel was truly a barrel then. But if you go further back in time, you will learn that most colonial homes had a piece of furniture used for this very same purpose—but it was not a barrel. Like so many other pieces from those bygone days, this, too, has been adapted to modern living for purposes far removed from the original. The piece in the photograph seen here is sure to arouse comment in any home. Its unusual silhouette and dimensions enclose a utility bin that is perfect for storing magazines, telephone books, boots and overshoes or even Mother's knitting.

To build the cracker barrel, cut all pieces to the size and shape indicated on the drawing. Assembly of the parts is simple, with only the lid offering any complications. Make the lid by gluing four ½ inch pine boards to a panel of ¼ inch plywood. Next, drill holes in the sides of the lid for the ¼ inch dowels which act as pivots. Coat the dowels with glue and insert them in the holes. Allow the glue to dry. The dowels fit into grooves cut in the pieces that form the sides of the cabinet. Make the grooves by drilling blind holes in the sides to the depth required for the dowels. Then, with a chisel, carefully extend the sides of the hole until a groove is formed that reaches to the top edge of the side piece. Now, assemble the cabinet. Nail and glue the sides to the back, then install the shelves and the front trim. With this done, the lid may be dropped into position by sliding the dowels down the grooves in the sides. Top trim and cabinet are then attached.

Choice of a finish for the wood is a matter of taste. Most prefer to have the warm, mellow look always associated with colonial furnishings. Antique pine stain, followed by a coat of paste wax, will give this effect. If a lighter finish is desired, the stain may be omitted and two coats of wax applied directly to the bare wood.

LIST OF MATERIALS

A. Two pieces, each 20¾"x23"x¾"
B. One piece, 20"x3"x¾"
C. One piece, 20"x2⅛"x¾"
D. Two pieces, each 7¾"x2¾"x¾"
E. One piece, 14¾"x18⅜"x¾"
F. One piece, 16"x22"x¾"
G. Two pieces, each 10"x2¾"x¾"
H. Two pieces, each 3¼"x14¾"x¾"
I. One piece, 10¾"x16¼"x¾"
J. Two pieces, each 16"x2¾"x¾"
K. One piece, 16¾"x18½"x¾"
L. One piece, 14½"x¾"x¾"
M. One piece, 16"x18½"x¾"
N. Three drawers, each: front, one piece, 5⅛"x 3¼"x¾"; side, two pieces, 13¼"x3¼"x½"; back, one piece, 4⅛"x3¼"x½"; bottom, one piece, 12¾"x4⅛"x½"
O. One drawer: front, one piece, 14½"x6"x¾"; side, two pieces, 16"x6"x¾"; back, one piece, 13"x6"x¾"; bottom, 13"x15¼"x¾" (not shown)
P. One piece, 20"x¾" molding
Q. Two pieces, each 14"x3¼"x¾"
R. One piece, 16⅞"x3¼"x¾"
S. One piece, 20¾"x18½"x¾"
T. One piece, 7"x18½"x¾"
¼" dia. dowels

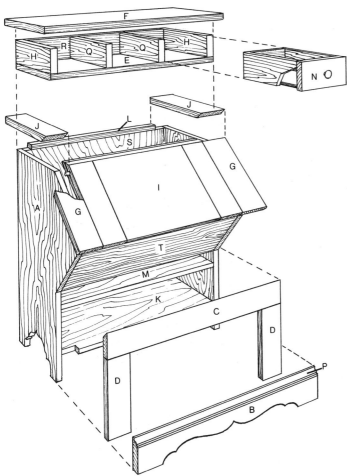

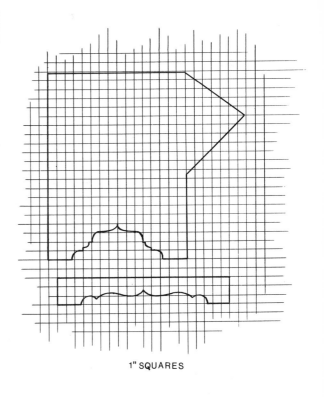

1" SQUARES

PROJECT 22—*SHAKER INFIRMARY CUPBOARD*

This two-door Shaker infirmary cupboard derived its name from its use in the communal infirmary during the active period of the religious sect's life in the United States more than a hundred years ago. Collectors today find many uses for this cupboard and its offbeat variations —among them, as a sideboard, server, storage cabinet and hallway display. Making it is a de-

light, for its construction is traditionally basic and sturdy.

You will want a soft finish, definitely not rich, as this is a lot of cupboard. So use a clear stock, something like pine, ash or maple, all of which will take a beautiful stain buffed to a lustrous finish.

Studying the sketch for a few minutes, you

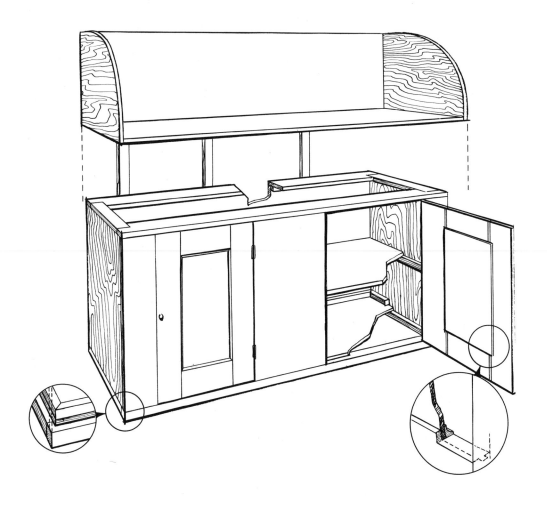

will see that the straight lines of the basic box are emphasized by a flush surface overall. The kickplate is flush, the doors are flush, and the board spacer just above the doors is flush. The only things that protrude are the beads of the hinges and the door pulls. Thus, in order to attach the sides, back and three front panels snug with the base frame, here is what you do:

First, make your rectangular base frame of 2x2 stock, butting the corners. Then cut your bottom shelf, allowing for the thickness of the front, back and sides; i.e., the shelf plus the sides, front and back should be equal to the outside dimensions of the base frame. Now add 1x1 stock to the top edge of the shelf, all around, but eliminate it at the door positions. Then center the shelf on the base frame and nail everything together. You now have a base with a rabbet-type groove all around to accommodate the bottom edges of the front, back and sides. Attach more 1x1 strips, this time to the top inside edges of the uprights. These will serve as strengtheners when you attach the flat board spacers around the top of the

basic box. Also, attach cleats for the center shelf at this time.

With the uprights prepared, install them, nailing the bottom edges into the 1x1's already attached to the shelf, and butt-nail the corners. This done, attach the board spacers around the top edges, using the rabbeted corner technique shown—but not before you lay the center shelf in position. Now you can install the front center panel, having allowed the exact spaces to the right and left for the doors. The top is made as a separate unit with a backboard and sides, and is secured directly to the board spacers with screws from the underside. Additionally, board strips attached to the backs of the top unit and the basic box strengthen the assembly.

The doors have inset panels (see the detail sketch), the frames being joined by tongue-and-groove method. Mortised hinges and button door pulls complete the job.

Because of the variation in the custom dimensions and option as to size, no list of materials is given for Shaker infirmary cupboard unit.

PROJECT 23—*EARLY AMERICAN HUTCH*

Of the dozens of early American furniture designs, no one piece seems to be more popular than the unassuming hutch. Utterly simple in detail yet highly serviceable no matter what the

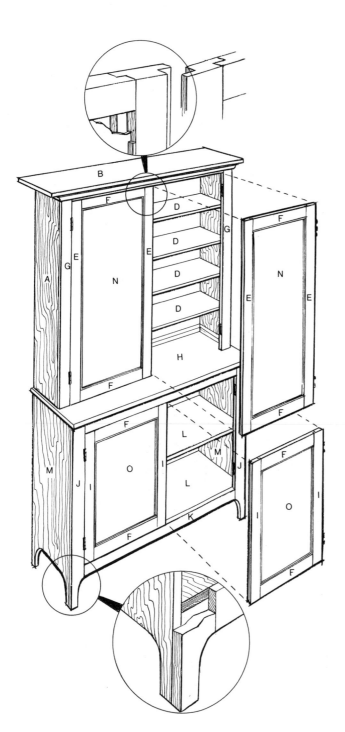

setting, the hutch is also a favorite of home craftsmen because it is a fast-moving project as well as a fine addition for any home. This one is an imposing piece (roughly 3x6 feet), so care should be taken in the selection of stock—nothing too rich or knotty. Stick to a clear ash or cherry or something warmish like spiced maple.

Taking a closer look at the hutch, you will notice the construction is a duplication process, the top being a slimmer version of the bottom or base cabinet. In our sample, the base extends only 12 inches from the wall, and the cabinet over it only 8 inches, providing a 4 inch setback at counter height. Making your own, you have the advantage of just about any personal modification you would care to bring about. If the sample seems too narrow for your needs, you can widen the base cabinet to 4 or 4½ feet. Or the total height can be reduced to 5½ or 5 feet in order to conform to other furnishings.

Construct two separate cabinets. Size and cut the four sides (note the cutaway on the base cabinet), the two tops, the two backs, and the bottom shelf for the base cabinet. Next, cut the three pieces of face trim for the top cabinet and the four pieces of trim for the base cabinet (note the cutaway portion of the two lengths of face trim that combine with the sides to form the front legs). Now assemble the boxes, nailing and gluing—nail through the sides into the bottom shelf. This done, attach the four shelves in the top cabinet and the middle shelf in the base cabinet. Attach the seven pieces of face trim, and, finally, the three lengths of cove molding (see sketch).

Join the top cabinet to the base cabinet with cleats as shown in the sketch. You will note that the door frames use rabbet joints throughout. Rabbets are also used for the frame edges where the two doors meet (see detail sketch), assuring a snug closure. The rabbet cuts serve as lips into which the doors' plywood panels are set, too.

Chip molding acts as a retainer strip for holding the panels in place.

Concealed spring catches, mortised hinges and decorative pulls make up the hardware.

LIST OF MATERIALS
A. Two pieces, each 41¼″x7¼″x¾″
B. One piece, 39″x10″x¾″
C. One piece, 33½″x27¾″x¼″ (not shown—back)
D. Four pieces, each 7″x33½″x¾″
E. Four pieces, each 39¾″x2½″x¾″
F. Eight pieces, each 11″x2½″x¾″
G. Two pieces, each 40½″x2½″x¾″
H. One piece, 36½″x14″x¾″
I. Four pieces, each 22¾″x2½″x¾″
J. Two pieces, each 30¾″x2½″x¾″
K. Two pieces, each 30″x2½″x¾″
L. Two pieces, each 33½″x11″x¾″
M. Two pieces, each 30¾″x11¼″x¾″
N. Two pieces, each 34¾″x10″x¼″
O. Two pieces, each 17¾″x10″x¼″
P. One piece, 41¼″x33½″x¼″ (not shown—back)
Q. One piece, 30″x1½″x¾″ (not shown—molding support strip)

cleats, 1½″ cove mold, and other moldings as required.

PROJECT 24—EARLY AMERICAN DRY SINK

Early American homes, being without plumbing, made do with the dry sink—a washstand for the bowl and water pitcher, and storage cabinet for related objects below. Today, these rare pieces are eagerly sought after by collectors, for they so readily adapt themselves to present-day usage in modern settings.

Except for the plywood back and door cleats, all pieces are cut from ¾ inch pine stock. Cut out all pieces to size and shape before starting assembly. Then attach top and bottom shelves to sides. Join with recessed screws, the holes being filled in with glued dowel pegs. The back is

attached to this assembly with flathead wood screws, set flush with the surface.

The top tray is next put together and attached to cabinet assembly with screws put up through the underside of the top shelf. Doors are constructed as sketched and attached with black iron butterfly hinges.

The drawers are easy to make according to sketch. The drawer glides—two narrow strips run from front to back at the drawer centerline—are installed. After drawers are fitted they are secured to glides with a screw and washer assembly. Drawer pulls are shaped with a wood rasp

LIST OF MATERIALS

A. One piece, 30″x33″x⅜″
B. Two pieces, each 15″x33″x¾″
C. Three pieces, each 15″x31½″x¾″
D. One piece, 34″x6″x¾″
E. One piece, 32½″x6″x¾″
G. Two pieces, each 16″x5″x¾″
H. One piece, 34″x4″x¾″
I. Two pieces, each 33″x7½″x¾″
J. One piece, 18⅜″x2″x¾″
K. One piece, 18⅜″x5½″x¾″
L. Two pieces, each 5½″x14¼″x¾″
M. One door, panel, one piece, 27⅞″x18⅜″x½″; side face, two pieces, 24⅞″x3″x¼″; bottom face, one piece, 12⅜″x3″x¼″; top face, one piece, 12⅜″x5″x¼″
N. Two drawers, each: front, one piece, 6″x4″x ¾″; front support, one piece, 5″x3″x½″; sides 13½″x3″x½″; back, one piece, 4″x3″x½″; bottom, one piece, 13½″x4″x½″

¾″x¾″ cleats as needed for support.

from dowel stock. Sand the entire cabinet and round edges with rasp and sandpaper irregularly for "antique" appearance.

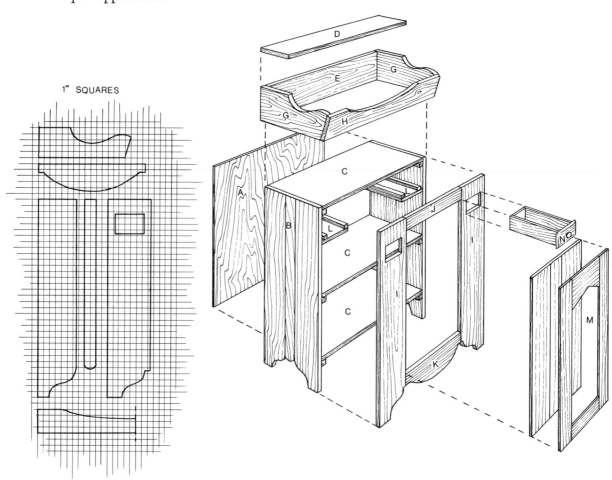

1″ SQUARES

PROJECT 25—
DRESSER/DRY SINK

This version of a Pennsylvania dresser with a dry sink dates to the mid-1700's.

The two sides of this dresser and dry sink can be cut from ¾ inch plywood, with wood tape used to cover the exposed edges, or preferably of boards glued and doweled together as shown in the cutting pattern. Join the sides with the shelves, sink top, drawer support, top, and back, gluing and nailing all joints. Dimensions of the upper sections can be varied to fit your purpose. The doors, with the original cabinetmaker's moldwork simplified for the handyman, are made

1" SQUARES

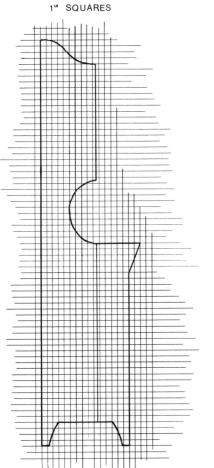

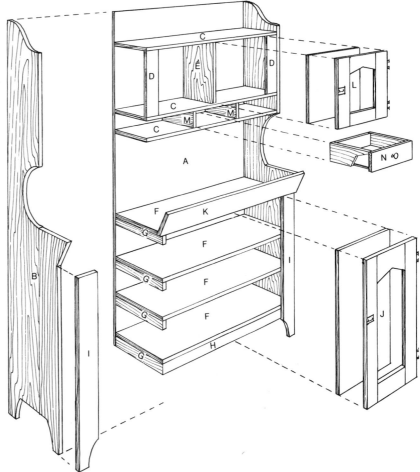

of ½ inch rails and stiles glued to ¼ inch plywood. A metal planter box is installed in the sink, or this area may be lined with plastic.

LIST OF MATERIALS
A. One piece, 68″x40″x½″
B. Two pieces, each 68″x17″x¾″
C. Three pieces, each 40″x9″x¾″
D. Two pieces, each 12″x4″x¾″
E. One piece, 12″x8¼″x¾″
F. Four pieces, each 40″x13¾″x¾″
G. Eight pieces, each 13¾″x1½″x¾″ (cleats)
H. One piece, 40″x1½″x¾″
I. Two pieces, each 29″x4¾″x¾″
J. Two doors, each: panel, one piece, 16″x 24″x ¼″; side face, two pieces, 24″x3″x½″; top face, one piece, 10″x6″x½″; bottom face, one piece, 10″x3″x½″
K. One piece, 41½″x6″x1″
L. Two doors, each: panel, one piece, 16″x 12″x¼″; side faces, two pieces, 16″x3″x½″; top face, one piece, 6″x5″x½″; bottom face, one piece, 6″x3″x½″
M. Two pieces, each 5½″x9″x¾″
N. Three drawers, each: front, one piece, 12½″x 5½″x¾″; sides, two pieces, 8¼″x5½″x½″; back, one piece, 11½″x5½″x½″; bottom, one piece, 7¾″x11½″x½″

PROJECT 26—DRY SINK WITH OPEN SHELVES

This Shaker unit is an especially interesting early American piece because it contains what could be one of the first iron sinks. Presumably cast in a Shaker foundry, with a drain in one end (which emptied into a bucket in the cupboard of the dry sink), it is, however, a feature you will probably want to forgo in your reproduction. With a practical substitute in mind, our plans show details for a recessed trough that can be copper- or tin-lined for use as a planter or to accommodate the traditional crockery basin.

The cupboard, sink and open shelves comprise the dry sink. First, assemble the sides, back and (enclosed) cupboard shelf, which is cleated, thus forming the base for the construction. Attach the two vertical pieces of face trim and the horizontal cross member. Prepare the trough separately, and slip it into place after attaching both the wide (left) and narrow (right) surface strips. Now you can secure the horizontal face trim and the molding under it.

Nail cleats to the sides in the open shelf section—two for the full-width shelf and one for the short shelf. Install the big shelf, then the upright divider (with its own cleat), and then the shorter shelf. Secure the top and the three-sided face trim, and the job is done except for the door.

The detail sketch shows how the door frame is rabbeted and inset with a panel and a stop strip. Note that a center strip has been added, creating a strong vertical effect. Hang the door with mortise hinges.

Regardless of your stock selection you can work up an excellent wood tone with any of the brush-on stains, buffing the surface vigorously until a rich luster is produced.

LIST OF MATERIALS

A. One piece, 45"x33½"x¾"
B. Two pieces, each 45"x20¾"x¾"
C. One piece, 35"x10¼"x¾"
D. One piece, 33"x9"x¾"
E. One piece, 16¼"x9"x¾"
F. One piece, 12"x9x¾"
G. One piece, 10¾"x6"x¾"
H. Two pieces, 10¾"x5"x¾"
I. One piece, 10¾"x2"x¾"
J. One piece, 35"x6"x1"
K. Two pieces, 23½"x5"x¾"

L. Two pieces, 20"x1"x¾"
M. One piece, 26½"x10"x¼"
N. One piece, 26½"x5¾"x¾"
O. One piece, 1"-quarter-round molding, 35"
P. One piece, flat molding, 31"
Q. One piece, 30"x19¾"x¾"
R. One door: side frames, two pieces, 24"x3"x¾"; bottom and top frames, two pieces, 19"x3"x¾"; center rail, one piece, 19"x1½"x¾"; panel, two pieces, 9"x19"x¼"; stop strip molding as needed.
S. Two pieces, each 12¾"x2"x½"
T. One piece, 25"x1½"x¾"
self cleats top upper not shown

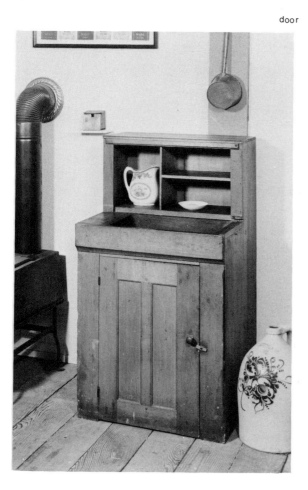

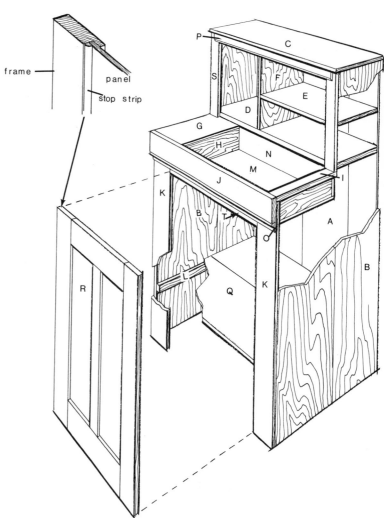

PROJECT 27—WATER BENCH

In the 1700's and early 1800's settlers in Pennsylvania favored this hutch-type water bench for service in the kitchen or bath, the enclosed lower half concealing jugs of reserve water and the waist-level top displaying the traditional pitcher and basin. At first glance, our model looks like a converted dry sink hutch, for a decorative back panel covers the usual see-through separation between the top and beveled small drawers. Either version, of course, makes the water bench a dandy conversation piece—as a sideboard, bar or vanity.

Dadoes are used for the small-drawer-shelf-network, with all other joints being butted-glued and nailed. For the sides, dowel and edge glue two boards or cut a single board, shaping the two cut-out areas of each side and rounded corner to suit. Attach the three sets of inner cleats to each side, add the bottom back, the notched bench top and the two inner shelves. This done, fasten a connecting cleat to the underside of the bench top, set back 1¼ inches from the front edge. Now secure the three door uprights to the front, later building the doors to the exact fit of the openings.

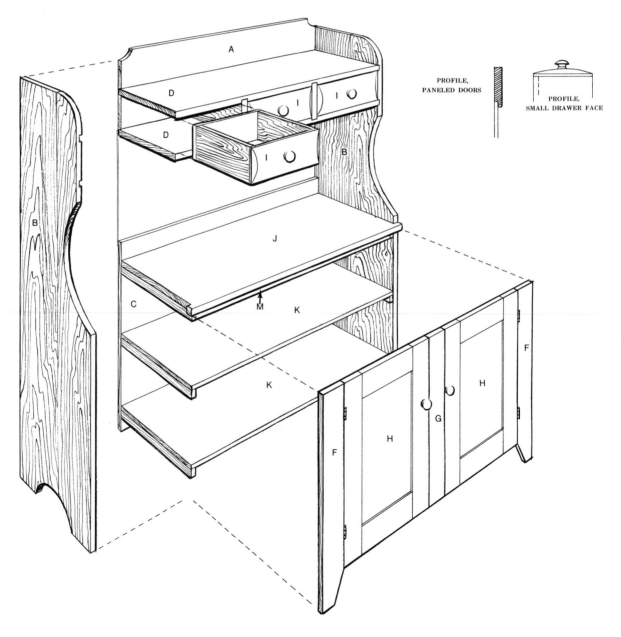

PROFILE,
PANELED DOORS

PROFILE,
SMALL DRAWER FACE

The top back panel and shelf network for the small drawers are next, the sides having been dadoed, as shown before reaching this stage.

At this point, you can elect to leave the midsection open—or decorate and install the midsection back panel. Our model shows a wallpaper-covered sheet of ¼ inch ply, overlapped and tacked into place. Finish off with door and drawer pulls, and spring or magnetic catches for the doors.

LIST OF MATERIALS

A. One piece, 39"x10"x¾"
B. Two pieces, each 52"x16¾"x1¼"
C. One piece, 39"x27½"x¾"
D. Two pieces, each 40"x12½"x1¼"
E. Two pieces, each 3"x12½"x1¼" (not shown)
F. Two pieces, each 24"x3"x¾"
G. One piece, 21"x3"x¾"
H. Two doors, each: side frames, two pieces, 21"x3"x¾"; top and bottom frames, two pieces, 9"x3"x¾"; panel 15"x9"x¼"
I. Three drawers, each: front, one piece, 12½"x 2½"x1¼"; sides, two pieces, 2"x2½"x½"; back, one piece, 11"x2½"x½"; bottom, one piece, 11½"x11"x¼"
J. One piece, 16¾"x41½"x1¼"
K. Two pieces, each 16"x39"x¾"
L. Six pieces, each 16"x2"x1" (cleats—not marked)
M. One piece, 35"x2"x1"

PROJECT 28—
EARLY AMERICAN STRAIGHT-BACK CHAIR

This early American chair is shown in the photo on the left and follows the basic chair construction described elsewhere in this book. The seat, however, is woven rush.

LIST OF MATERIALS

C. Two pieces, each 45"x1¾" diameter
A. Two pieces, each 19"x1¾" diameter
B. Six pieces, each 15"x¾" diameter
D. Three pieces, each 18"x¾" diameter
E. Two pieces, each 15"x¾" diameter
F. One piece, 15¼"x4"x½"
G. One piece, 15¼"x3½"x½"
H. One piece, 15¼"x3"x½"

PROJECT 29—*SHAKER DRY SINK*

You would hardly use a dry sink for washing with today's plumbing—but a dry sink functions beautifully as a planter. Not only is there space for a pleasing arrangement of plants on its upper surface, but it also offers more than adequate storage space for gardening tools and other items in its large and roomy interior. The towel rack retains its usefulness and offers a beautiful contrast to the humdrum racks you see today.

This dry sink and towel rack is a pleasing combination that reflects two basic tenets of the Shaker faith—unity and simplicity. The method of building the dry sink and towel rack, once the wood is cut, is obvious from the drawing. Patterns for shaping the top of the sides of the dry sink (F) and the base of the towel rack (P) are given on the left on 1-inch squares.

Three basic types of joints are used to build

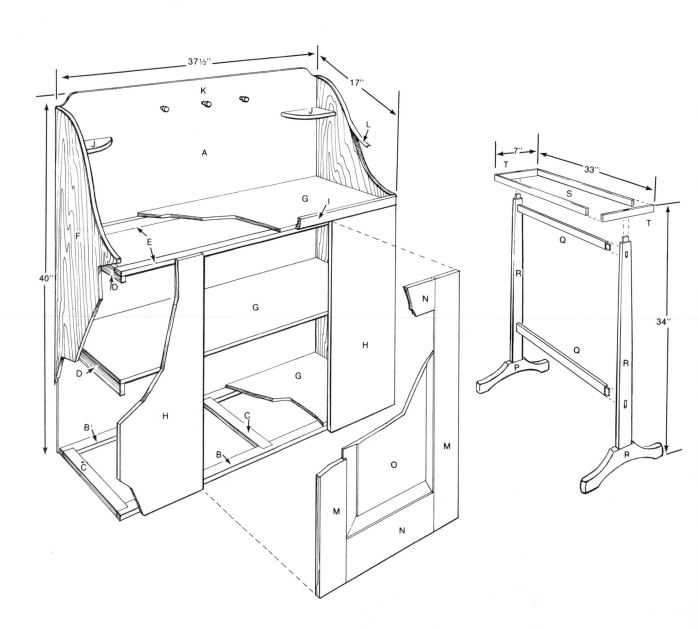

both pieces. Most of them are simple butt joints, but the back and sides as well as the frame of the dry sink use rabbet joints. The center cross pieces of the frame (C) are dadoed into the longer side pieces (B). Close examination of the detail of the door will show that the center piece (O) is rabbeted flush with the back of the door. As for the towel rack, all the joints with the exception of the top pieces (S, T) are mortise and tenon. And of these mortise and tenon joints, all of them are open with the exception of those joining the two uprights (R) to the base (P). All the joints in both pieces are nailed and glued.

Solid stock is used for both pieces. The use of wood strips or possibly wood tape (L) to cover the edges of the sides of the dry sink is optional. Although the original of both pieces is pine with a yellow stain, you can work up an excellent wood tone with any of the brush-on stains, buffing the surface until a soft luster is produced.

LIST OF MATERIALS

A. One piece, 40″x37½″x⅜″
B. Two pieces, each 36″x3″x1″
C. Three pieces, each 13⅝″x3″x1″
D. Four cleats, each 16⅝″x2″x1″
E. Two pieces, each 36″x2″x1″
F. Two pieces, each 40″x17½″x¾″
G. Three pieces, each 36″x16⅝″x½″
H. Two pieces, each 24″x7¹¹⁄₁₆″x1″
I. One piece, 37½″x2″x1″
J. Two pieces, each 6″x6″x1″
K. Three pegs, each 4″x1″ diameter
L. Two pieces of laminate, each 25″x¾″x¹⁄₁₆″
M. Two pieces, each 24″x4″x1″
N. Two pieces, each 23⅞″x11″x4″
O. One piece, 16″x11″x1″
P. Two pieces, each 15″x4½″x1″
Q. Two pieces, each 33″x2″x1″
R. Two pieces, each 29½″x3″x1″
S. Two pieces, each 31″x1¼″x1″
T. Two pieces, each 7″x1¼″x1″

PROJECT 30—*STORAGE CUPBOARD*

This piece is typical of Shaker storage units: it is big. The Shakers lived community-style, and it was important to conserve space; one large unit, which many people could share, was more desirable than a number of smaller ones. In a sense, the sharing of the piece was also a reflection of the Shaker philosophy of unity.

You can build this piece with plywood, solid stock, or a combination of the two. We recommend both plywood and solid stock in our construction because it allows a number of shortcuts, among which are fewer exposed plywood edges that have to be covered by wood strips or wood tape.

Start by making the sides of random-width boards doweled and edge-glued together with

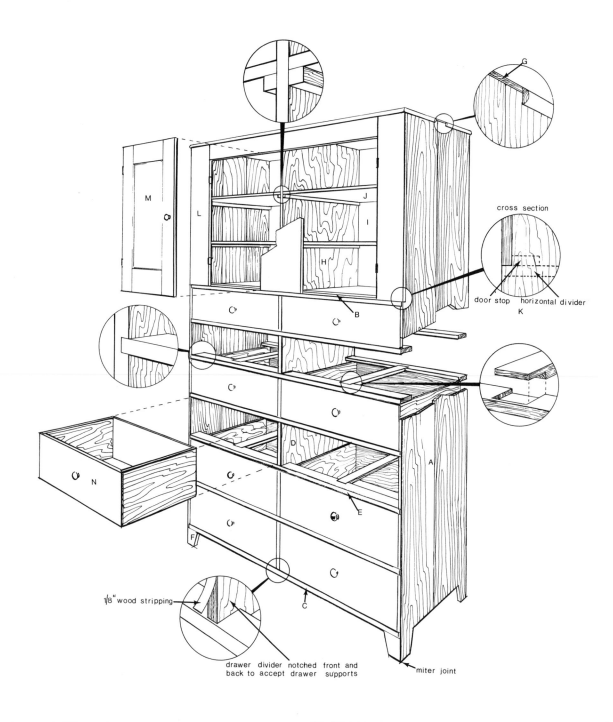

cross section

door stop   horizontal divider
K

1/8" wood stripping

drawer divider notched front and back to accept drawer supports

miter joint

down through the cupboard-drawer divider into its top edge; its notched bottom corners fit onto the bottom drawer supports. Now, attach the rest of the drawer supports.

Next, attach the top, the piece that divides the cupboard shelves, and the shelves. You can install the back next; it is composed of pieces of ¼ inch plywood cut from a 4x8 panel. The sections should be installed horizontally and butted together with the edges fitting into rabbet cuts made in the back edges of both sides.

Drop in the shelves on their cleats as shown, and install the 1x2 strips which serve as door stops. Attach the cupboard facing pieces. Next, hang the doors and fit the drawers, and nail on the molding strips around the top edges. Then you can attach the feet in the front of the unit to the sides using miter joints. Finally, cover all exposed plywood edges with wood tape or ⅛ inch thick strips to match the wood you have chosen. In our construction we used ⅛ inch stripping, and the dimensions reflect this.

LIST OF MATERIALS

A. Two sides composed of random-width boards. Each 78¼"x18"x¾"

B. One cupboard-drawer divider, plywood, 49¼"x17¾"x¾"

C. Bottom drawer support, 1x2's cut to fit

D. One drawer divider, plywood, 49½"x17¾"x ¾"

E. Five 1"x2" drawer supports, cut to fit

F. Two front feet, 3½" high, tapered, 2¾" at top, 2" at the bottom x¾"

G. One top, 50"x18"x¼"

H. One cupboard divider, plywood, 28"x17"x¾"

I. One back, 74¾"x49¼"x¼"

J. Four cupboard shelves, ¼ or ½ inch plywood, cut to fit

K. Two door stop strips, 1x2's cut to fit

L. Four facing pieces for cupboard. Two stiles, each 28"x5"x¾"; one middle member, 24⅜"x 11"x¾"; one crosspiece, 40"x3¾"x¾"

M. Two doors, plywood, each 24⅜"x14½"x¾"

N. Twelve drawers. Use ¾ inch face stock

the feet cut out as shown. Then cut the recesses in the sides which will accept the drawer support ends. Also make dado cuts in both sides to accept the piece of plywood that divides the drawers from the cupboard.

Now, slip the drawer-cupboard divider into the dado cuts and glue it in place. This produces an H-shaped structure.

Next, install the bottom drawer support, fitting the ends into the precut recesses, installing the crosspieces with lap joints as shown in the detail drawing. With this support in place, you can attach the piece of ply that divides the drawers vertically. This piece is notched, as shown, to accept the front and rear members of the other drawer support. You can attach it by screwing

PROJECT 31—*CORNER CABINET*

A unique piece is this classically simple corner cabinet that found so much favor in the early days.

It is not uncommon for a room corner to be somewhat out of square, so it would be wise to check the proposed location for the corner cabinet before construction and make any necessary adjustments in angle so that the sides will fit tightly against the wall. Or, if you prefer, you may make the cabinet corner angle slightly ob-

tuse, on speculation that it may not always be placed in a square corner. Because of differing dimensions in a home, a list of materials is not included with this project. Instead approximate dimensions are given on the working drawing.

Begin the construction by attaching the ¼ inch plywood sides to the shelves, gluing and nailing through the sides. Then attach the beveled front pieces, the trim, and the top. The door is hung with butt hinges.

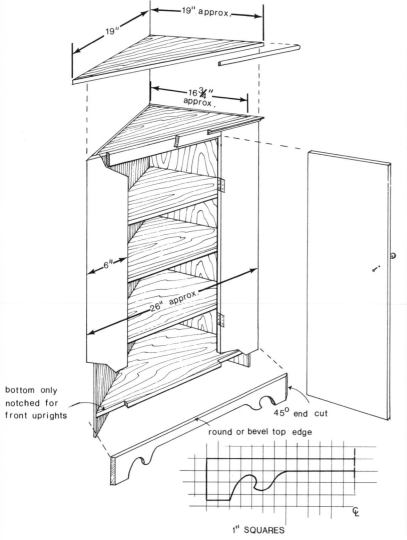

19" approx.

19"

16¾" approx.

6"

26" approx.

bottom only
notched for
front uprights

45° end cut

round or bevel top edge

1" SQUARES

PROJECT 32—*COLONIAL SIX-BOARD CHEST*

In more than its age this lovely example of the cabinetmaker's art is a reminder of days gone by. The very boards from which it was made are relics of a time when our country was young and its forests old, full of pines grown straight and tall and of a girth unseen today. From these huge old trees, boards the width of those used here were sawed—and some far wider. Today they are almost impossible to come by, unless one goes to great trouble and expense. Despite this obstacle, however, the chest may be duplicated by either of two methods. Both give good results; one is perhaps a bit easier. The latter requires the use of pine-veneered plywood, which introduces a problem of its own—disguising the plywood at the edges of the dovetails. These can, of course, be covered with flexible wood tape, a slow, tedious task. The other method avoids this problem but introduces an additional step. You make your own wide boards by doweling and edge-gluing narrow planks.

Regardless of which path you choose, the construction then follows the same procedure, with the various components going together as seen in the drawing. Except for cutting the dovetails, no difficulties should be encountered. Even here, some irregularity may be countenanced for, if you look at the photo carefully, you will see six dovetails on the right side of the chest, and seven on the other.

LIST OF MATERIALS

A. Two pieces, each 39½"x17"x1"

B. Two pieces, each 18½"x17"x1"

C. One piece, 39½"x18½"x1"

D. Four pieces, each 4"x4"x4"

E. One piece, 39½"x18½"x1"

F. One piece, 41½"x1¼"x1"

G. Two pieces, each 18½"x1¼"x1"

H. Two pieces, each 16½"x8"x¾"

I. One piece, 16½"x6"x¾"

J. One piece, 41½" long, 1" quarter-round molding

K. Two pieces, 19½" long, 1" quarter-round molding

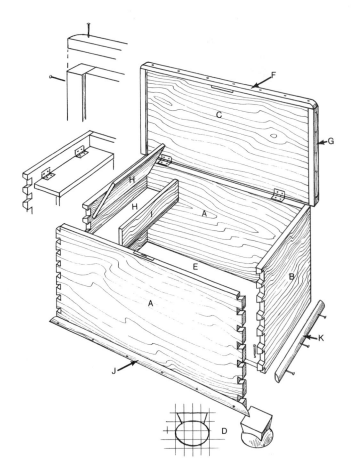

PROJECT 33—*EARLY AMERICAN CHEST OF DRAWERS*

This chest is free of any ornament other than the cutout base and the split-spindle decorations on the two corner posts. Its purpose is strictly one of utility but its beauty is in its simplicity of design. Almost all the space occupied by the chest is given over to storage. For this reason alone it is worth reproducing the original colonial piece shown here for a modern-size bedroom where storage space is always at a premium.

Construction is basically simple although—as was usual in colonial times—economy in lumber was not considered. The reproduction may make use of plywood for economy's sake in those sections not exposed to view. The back, too, may be ¼ inch plywood in a single piece. For example, drawer bottoms may be ¼ inch plywood or hardboard, and the solid boards on which the drawers slide may be plywood with a solid-wood facing strip.

Start by cutting pieces to size, and join the pieces necessary for the solid-wood top by use of glue and dowels to make the single wide piece of the top. Its edges are then rounded with a wood rasp and sanded smooth. Attach ends to posts, then join ends by insertion of the drawer supports which are cut out to fit around corner posts. Attach cleats or guides to drawer supports. Then mount the assembled cabinet on the base, and add the top. Drawers are then made separately and trimmed to fit. Round all exposed edges irregularly with coarse, then fine, sandpaper.

Finally, cut in half a spindle (which may be an ornamental stairway baluster or buy an ornamental piece of molding that fits the colonial design) and attach to the end posts with glue and brads.

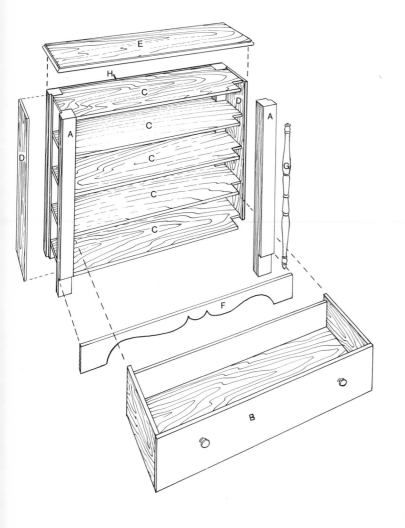

LIST OF MATERIALS (Project 33)

A. Four pieces, each 41″x2⅝″x2⅝″

B. Four drawers, each: front, one piece, 42¾″x 7⅞″x¾″; sides, two pieces, 7⅞″x14¾″x¾″; back, one piece, 41¼″x5⅞″x¾″; bottom, one piece, 41¼″x14¾″x¼″; drawer pulls, two pieces, 1½″ diameter.

C. Five pieces, each 46½″x15¾″x¾″

D. Two pieces, each 41″x12¾″x¾″

E. One piece, 49″x16½″x¾″

F. One piece, 48″x5½″x¾″

G. One piece, 34″x1⅞″ (approximate)

H. One piece, 42¾″x41″x¼″

PROJECT 34—*COLONIAL BED CHEST* (*for picture see page 60*)

When the original of this chest was created years ago, the gracefully molded edges were formed with hand tools that—quite frequently—had to be made first before work could begin. Your reproduction of the antique pine chest takes advantage of stock moldings from your lumber dealer.

Start with the simple framework of sides and top and bottom rails. The sides may be rabbeted at the back edges for insertion of a ¼ inch plywood back which will stiffen the piece. Assemble the dividers, drawer glides and corner braces as single units and then attach to sides with glue and screws.

Cut out the base supports and attach to the chest with glue and finishing nails, counterset. Base molding goes on next with glue and brads. Attach the crown moldings with glue and brads, then attach the top with glue and brads put through the crown molding. Counterset all brads.

Construct three drawers as shown. Bottom may be held in place by cleats. Attach the beveled pine panels with glue and brads, then add the drawer pulls.

LIST OF MATERIALS

A. One piece, 36″x11½″x¾″

B. One piece, 20″x33″x¼″

C. Two pieces, each 20″x10¾″x¾″

(*continued on page 108*)

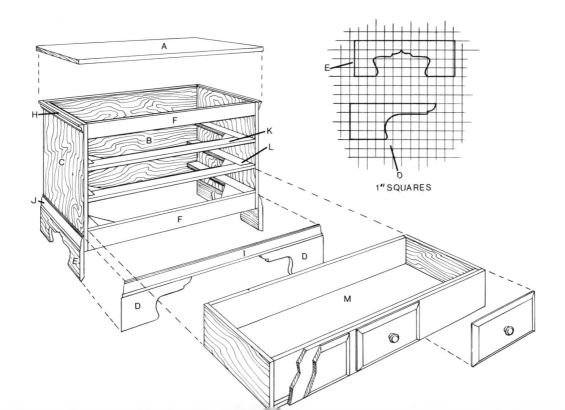

1″SQUARES

D. Two pieces, each 4"x10"x¾"

E. Two pieces, each 4"x11½"x¾"

F. Two pieces, each 33"x2¼"x¾"

G. One piece, 36"x¾" crown molding (not shown)

H. Two pieces, each 11½"x¾" crown molding

I. One piece, 36"x¾" base molding

J. Two pieces, each 11½"x¾" base molding

K. Two pieces, each 33"x2½"x¾"

L. Six pieces, each 10"x2½"x¾"

M. Three drawers, each: sides, two pieces 10"x 4⅜"x½"; back and front, two pieces, 31½"x 3⅜"x½"; front, one piece, 33"x4⅜"x½"; front panels, three pieces, 10⅜"x4⅜"x½"; bottom, one piece, 31½"x10"x½" corner blocks

glue blocks as needed.

PROJECT 35—*BLANKET CHEST*

The chest, in one form or another, is a very old article of furniture, for a homemaker's need of out-of-the-way storage knows no era. The one pictured (*see page 60*) is of a type common in New England during the early 1700's; chests with drawers were becoming increasingly popular, but the deep upper compartment with hinged lid was often retained. Yellow pine and white pine were favorite woods, although many ornate and intricately carved samples in oak were often to be found in homes located in the steadily growing urban areas.

The charmingly hand-carved wall decoration graced the peak of the gable end of a Pennsylvania Dutch home. Its harmonious design reflects the Germanic love of order and symmetry. The central motif is the tree of life, but the significance of some of the other features—such as the two flanking flowerpots and the blossom at the treetop—is less clear. Duplication of this unique ornamentation might be a satisfying leisure-time project for the artistically inclined woodworker.

Cut the two side panels, using a sabre saw or coping saw to shape the scroll patterns. Cut the front legs and attach these to the sides with glue and 6d finishing nails. Fasten cleats between the sides at rear top and bottom, then attach the ¼ inch plywood back to cleats and side panels with glue and 4d finishing nails. Glue and nail the lower and intermediate drawer glides and front dividers in place. Nail through sides and back to attach the plywood bottom of the upper compartment. Now glue and nail the front panel in

place. Fasten molding at the ends of the lid, then secure this to the rear cleat with concealed hinges.

Construct the drawer frames (the lower is 6½ inches, the upper, 6 inches) and attach cleats, then fit the plywood drawer bottoms. Finish the piece before attaching antique drawer pulls. The character marks—scratches and nicks accumulated during long years of faithful service—may

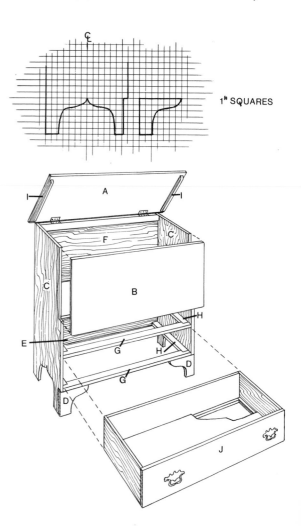

1" SQUARES

be carefully simulated, if you wish, by judicious gouging and scarring.

LIST OF MATERIALS

A. One piece, 35″x14¾″x¾″
B. One piece, 33½″x16″x¾″
C. Two pieces, each 36″x14″x¾″
D. Two pieces, each 7″x6″x¾″
E. One piece, 32″x14¼″x¾″
F. One piece, 32″x30″x¼″
G. Two pieces, 32″x2½″x¾″
H. Four pieces, 13″x2½″x¾″
 I. Two pieces, 13¼″x¾″x¾″
 J. Two drawers, each: front, one piece 32″x6½″x ¾″; sides, two pieces, 13¼″x6½″x¾″; back, one piece, 30½″x6½″x¾″; bottom, one piece, 12½″x30½″x¼″; side cleats, two pieces, 11″x ¾″x½″; front-back cleats, two pieces, 30½″x ¾″x½″

PROJECT 36—*SHAKER BED*

This Shaker bed is extremely simple in its basic structure. The side rails (D) and cross pieces (C) are joined to the legs (A-B) in simple butt joints reinforced with strong steel bolts six inches long and ½ inch thick.

Holes for the bolts are drilled through the square part of the legs and into the end grain of the side rails and cross pieces. Another hole is then drilled at right angles to the lengthwise hole to provide space for the insertion of the nut and its washer shown in the detail. Of course, you can simply use a long lag bolt which requires no nut, but a machine bolt and nut has more holding power than a lag bolt. The head of the bolt must be countersunk and the round opening enlarged with a chisel or router to form a rectangular shape for a plug to cover the hole in the

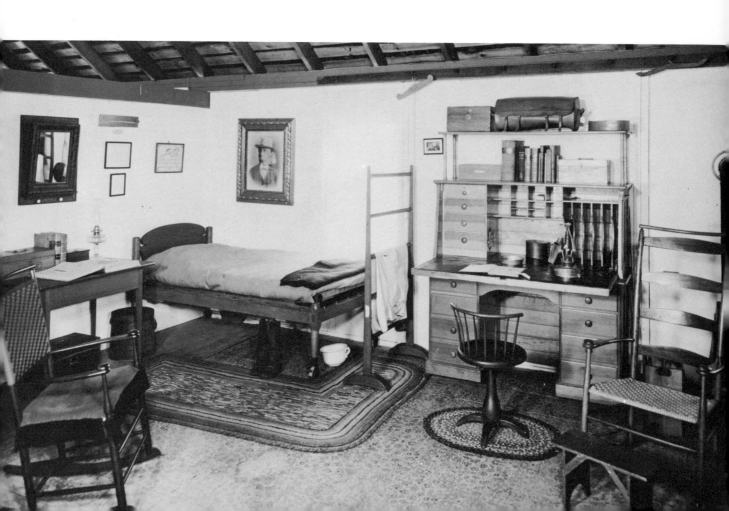

leg. The plug need only be about ¼ inch thick and should be cut from end grain so that it will stain darker than the surrounding wood and look like a plug.

The little pegs on the top of the bed frame were originally used to anchor ropes that were laced back and forth across the width and down the length of the frame. The ropes, of course, functioned as "springs" for the mattress. The cleats (F) on the inside of the rails (D) are supposed to support a bedspring. The usual box spring, which is about 6 inches high should not be used here because it will raise the mattress too far above the rails. The flat type of spring commonly used in metal folding cots is best for the purpose.

The headboard (G) should be cut from a piece of ¾ inch plywood, preferably with a birch veneer facing. Use birch veneer tape to conceal the edges of the plywood. Note the two points on each side of the headboard which form tenons that engage slots in the upper parts of the adjacent legs. Note also that the legs at the foot of the bed are really the same as those next to the headboard except for the round upper extensions. (See leg detail.) Since the casters cannot be duplicated, it is suggested that modern 4 inch casters be used.

LIST OF MATERIALS

A. Two pieces, each 18″x3½″x3½″
B. Two pieces, each 39″x3½″x3½″
C. Two pieces, each 37½″x3″x3″
D. Two pieces, each 72″x3″x3″
E. Thirty-two pieces, each ¾″ dia. x 1½″
F. Four pieces, each 8″x1″x1″
G. One piece, 41″x21″x¾″
H. 8 bolts 6x½″, 8 nuts, 16 washers
I. ¾″ veneer strip
J. Eight pieces, each 2″x1¼″x¼″

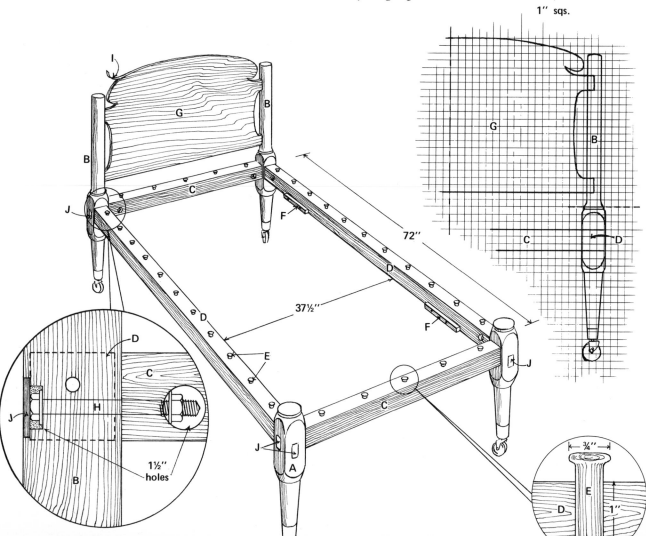

PROJECT 37—*COLONIAL BED*

Although this early American bed requires a great deal of lathe work, the basic construction is the same as the preceding project. In this one, however, the mattress spring is held in position by a five-foot piece of 1½"x1½" angle iron. This support is fastened to both side pieces (B). The scroll work for the head may be cut with a scroll or band saw. If a double bed is desired, pieces (C), (E) and (F) should be increased to 54" and 56½", respectively.

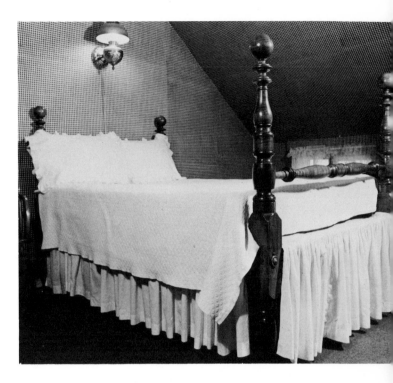

LIST OF MATERIALS

A. Four pieces, each 50"x4"x4"
B. Two pieces, each 80"x3½"x3"
C. Two pieces, each 38"x3½"x3"
D. Two pieces, each 1½"x1½" angle iron, 60" long
E. One piece, 40½"x2"x2"
F. One piece, 40½"x15½"x¾"
G. Bolts (eight 8"x½"), dowels as needed

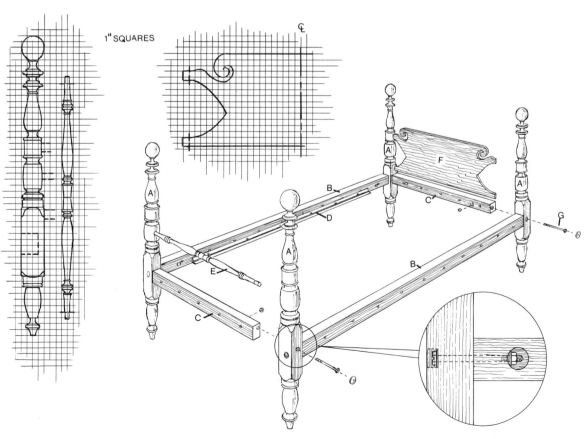

PROJECT 38—*FOUR-POSTER BED*

The construction of this four-poster early American bed is basically the same as Project 36 and Project 37. It receives its colonial pegged effect by using one-inch dowels flattened as shown in the detailed drawing.

LIST OF MATERIALS

A. Four pieces, each 50″x4″x4″
B. Two pieces, each 80″x4″x3″
C. Two pieces, each 38″x4″x3″
D. Two pieces, each 1½″x1½″ angle iron, 60″ long
E. Thirty-eight pieces, each 1½″x1″ diameter dowels
F. One piece, 40½″x19½″x¾″
G. Eight pieces, 8″x½″ bolts

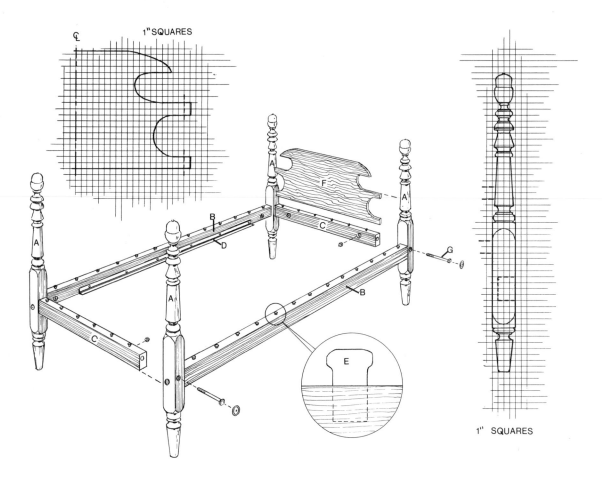

PROJECT 39—
COUNTING DESK VANITY

Whenever one of the majestic square-rigger merchantmen of early America hove into view in mid-channel, a longboat was immediately put over the side bearing a junior officer who was steered with all dispatch to the bustling dockside. Within minutes, he would present himself at the shipping firm's counting house, standing ramrod straight before the counting desk of his employers, where he would hand over the ship's manifest, thus officially concluding another great sea voyage.

How many transactions these proper little counting desks have participated in will never be known, but the clean lines and utter simplicity of their design did make them a long-time favorite of busy merchants—and possibly even some junior officers. Made of pine and butternut (walnut) stock, this counting desk may serve in

the den, or, as shown here, as a vanity with flip-top mirror. The stock is predominantly ¾ inch; exceptions include ½ inch thickness for the small drawers, their shelves and the shelf within the box, and ¼ inch stock for the upright separators and the drawer bottoms.

All joints are butt type, glued and then secured with screws. All screw holes are plugged. The desk top (20x32), backboard (10x33½) and hinged lid are all doweled and edge-glued, as required.

1" SQUARES

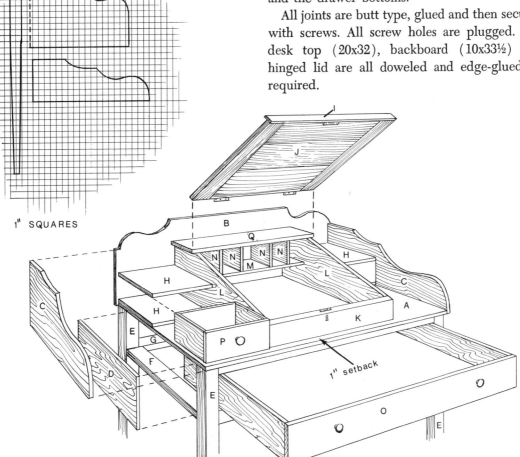

1" setback

Begin assembly with the four legs and five spacers, four of which are bottom supports for the big drawer. Then, secure the desk top with glue and screws in the legs and the one upper drawer spacer. When this is done, add the lower side panels, recessing them between the front and back legs. Next, fasten the two diagonal sides of the box to the desk top, allowing an inch setback in the front and ¾ inch space in the back. You can now add the backboard and the front panel containing the lock (see your hardware supply dealer for the correct type). Then, screw the four shelves for the small drawers into place, the top shelves through the backboard and the box uprights. These can be followed with the upper side panels.

Preassemble the exterior and interior box shelves, including the separators; slip the entire unit into place within the box, against the backboard. Fit the hinged lid, making sure alignment with its base and the lock is correct. Install a lid support to hold the lid/mirror in an open position.

LIST OF MATERIALS

A. One piece, 32″x20″x¾″
B. One piece, 33½″x10″x¾″
C. Two pieces, each 20″x7″x¾″
D. Two pieces, each 16″x6½″x¾″
E. Four pieces, each 31″x2″x2″
F. Two pieces, each 16″x2″x¾″
G. Two pieces, each 28″x2″x¾″
H. Four pieces, each 8″x7″x½″
 I. One piece, 19″x1″x¾″
J. One piece, 19″x20″x¾″
K. One piece, 18″x3½″x¾″
L. Two pieces, each 9″x20″x¾″
M. One piece, 16½″x6″x½″
N. Four pieces, each 6″x6″x½″
O. One drawer: front, one piece, 28″x5″x¾″; sides, two pieces, 20″x5″x½″; back, one piece, 26½″x5″x½″; bottom, one piece, 26″x19½″x½″
P. Two drawers, each: front, one piece, 7″x3″x½″; sides, two pieces, 7½″x3″x½″; back, one piece, 6″x3″x½″; bottom, one piece, 7″x6″
Q. One piece, 19″x6″x¾″

PROJECT 40—WRITING DESK

A slightly older and slightly more elaborate variation of Project 39, this original and finely done piece is a study in simplicity and orderliness. The desk is all business, both as a finished piece and in the shop. Studying the sketch against the photo, you will see the two important features you do not want to miss: the molding strips at the edge of the desk top and flip-top, and the more subtle molding on the underside of the front panel or facing. The particular idea with the underside molding is to give that edge a somewhat flared appearance—slight lip or trim that helps to add a well-finished look.

Other than these two points, the concealed, flip-top compartments behind the flip-top desk top need special mention. All there is to it is a shelf positioned at the halfway mark (the full pigeon-hole to the right or left is 4¼ inches), with a face, dividers and top added. This shelf also serves as the base or support for the larger, hinged desk top. The short space in the rear is regarded simply as an extension of the general stationery storage under the flip-top.

Turn the four legs on a lathe following the profile shown on the inch-square graph and then groove each of the leg tops twice—in this case, ¼″x½″x5½″ (you will want to partially plug the two grooves which will show when either of the drawers are pulled open). Precut the front panel for the drawers, assembling it, the two side panels, one back panel and four legs. Now is a good time to install the rails (and their supports) for the drawers. Attach the 24x38½ top (dowel and edge-glue). Thus far, you've got a table, and can now go on to the desk appointments.

Prepare the two central dividers, notched and beveled, and dowel and edge-glue them to the top. Add the central connecting shelf, and skip on to the two decorative sides. Note that the front ends are notched (see graph) to accept the top molding mentioned earlier. Glue and nail them to the edges of the top, attach the full-width, upper back panel, and the two matched top shelves that connect the decorative sides to the central dividers. Having put the small facing panel on the central halfway shelf, you can start inserting the little upright dividers to suit your fancy.

What now remains to be done is the short flip-top for the back compartments, the hinged desk top (secured directly to the small, facing panel), the top molding (which should protrude beyond the molding to the right and left), and the underside molding. Make the drawers in the classic butt-joint style of the time, and consult your hardware supplier or a locksmith for the lock type on the hinged top/facing panel.

LIST OF MATERIALS

A. Two pieces, each 24½"x6"x¾"
B. One piece, 24"x38½"x¾"
C. Four pieces, each 28¼"x2"x2"
D. Two pieces, each 21"x5½"x½"
E. Two pieces, each 12½"x9"x½"
F. Two pieces, each 15"x9"x½"
G. One piece, 16"x15"x¾"

H. Two pieces, each 24½"x5¼"x¾"
I. One piece, 38½"x5½"x½" (not shown)
J. Two pieces, 37"x5½"x½"
L. Two pieces, each 24"x4½"x¾" (not shown)
M. Twelve pieces, each 24"x½"x½" (slides—not marked)
N. Four pieces, each 6"x8⅞"x½"
O. One piece, 15"x2½"x½"
P. Three pieces, each 9"x2½"x½"
Q. One piece, 40"x¾" half-round molding (desk front—not marked)
R. Two drawers, each: front, one piece, 9"x3½"x¾"; sides, two pieces, 22¼"x3½"x½"; back, 8"x3½"x½"; bottom, one piece, 21¾"x8"x½"

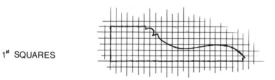

1" SQUARES

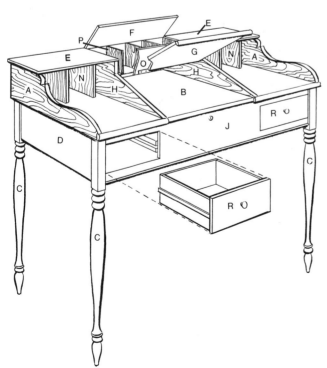

1" SQUARES

PROJECT 41—*SHAKER WRITING DESK*

The small size of this desk suggests that it was used by a woman and that she occupied a position of authority in the Shaker community, because during this time only a leader would have use for a desk. The average Shaker was not permitted to write to the "outside world"—for fear of his secularization—and this and other writing chores fell to the few individuals in authority.

The original is of butternut stock, a yellowish white wood available today only at prohibitive prices. So, just build it in the kind of wood you like using, boards or plywood. We have chosen plywood for the simplest, most economical construction. The dimensions are faithful to the original, except for a few which have been adapted to plywood stock to be used for most parts.

For construction, think of the piece as a table with a storage compartment on top of it, and a separate storage unit with cubbyholes on top of this.

Make the table first, connecting front, back and sides to the posts with blocks as shown in the drawing, then screw-block on a middle bracing member between the inside faces of the front and back for strength. Attach small blocks as indicated for nailing on the inside ends of the drawer tracks. Fit the drawers and screw on the one-piece table top. Preassemble the front and sides of the storage compartment—by dovetailing or butt screwing—and attach it to the table top by driving screws up through the projecting lip of the table top into its bottom edges. Screw on the storage compartment top, then hinge on the lift-up lid. Next, screw the preassembled cubbyhole storage unit to the top of the other storage compartment and attach the one-piece

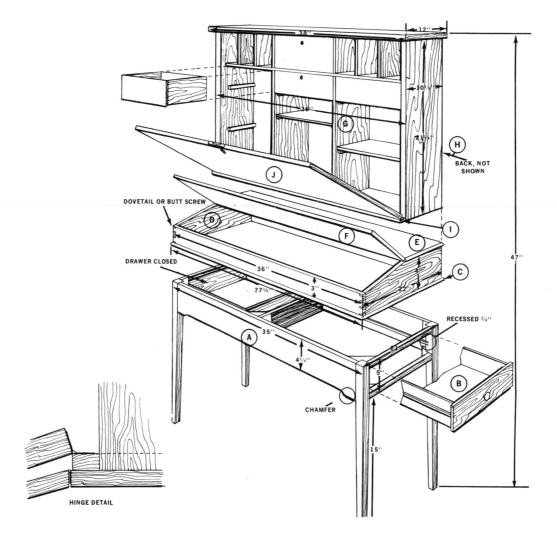

back to both. Screw on the long strip flush with front base of the cubbyhole unit and hinge the drop-down lid to this strip. Bevel the edges of the table top and the top and lid of the lower storage compartment. Cover exposed edges with wood tape to match the plywood you use and finish to suit.

LIST OF MATERIALS

A. One table: legs, four pieces 20"x2"x2"; front and back, two pieces, 31"x5"x¾"; side braces, four pieces, 17½"x1"x1"; middle brace, one piece, 20"x5"x¾"

B. Two drawers: side to fit using ¾" stock

C. One piece, 37½"x22¾"x½"

D. Lift-up top storage compartment; front, one piece, 36"x3"x¾"; sides, two pieces, 22"x4"x ¾" trimmed to accept lift-up top.

E. One piece, 37½"x11¼"x½"

F. One piece, 37½"x12"x½"

G. Cubbyhole storage unit: sides, two pieces, 21¼"x10⅜"x¾"; top, one piece, 38"x12"x¾"; bottom, one piece, 34½"x10⅜"x½"; cut cubbyholes and drawers to fit using ¼" plywood.

H. One piece, 36"x26¼"x½"

I. One piece, 36"x¾"x½"

J. One piece, 36"x20¾"x¾"

PROJECT 42—
MERCHANT'S DESK

Once a sturdy work desk in a mercantile establishment, this large handsome piece bears the scars of its long years of service. Some surfaces are distressed, and the front edge of the top shows nail holes where there once must have been fastened a small lip that prevented ledgers from sliding to the floor. Because of the desk's generous dimensions, a large room would be its best setting. To fit your scale of living, however, a smaller version may be desirable. The piece is easily reduced, losing none of its authentic look in the transition. Elimination of one drawer and minor reduction of the front-to-back dimension and leg thickness are recommended.

The original, with its liberal use of dadoes and mortise-and-tenon joints, shows the builder's careful attention to detail. Those who wish to duplicate its original condition will want to know there is evidence that another 2x4 once stretched from one side 2x4 to the other; this is not shown on the plans.

With all parts cut, construction is quite simple. Assemble one front and one rear leg with its side and 2x4 brace; glue and clamp. When dry, fit the front 1x4 horizontal members and back panel in their dadoes, glue and clamp. With the main framework now constructed, the drawer separators and drawer slides can be screwed and glued in. It is suggested that the drawers be cut and fitted next, as access to the interior is, of course, much easier before the top is attached.

The sloping top is made from two pieces of clear 1x12 pine, doweled and edge-glued, cut to 20 inches deep. The forward edge of the horizontal shelf across the back of the top is mitered to the angle which is formed by the back edge of the 20 inch piece with vertical. Seal the undersides and edges of the top before attaching, to prevent warping. Several coats of thinned shellac will suffice.

The final construction step is attaching the

LIST OF MATERIALS

A. Two pieces, each 30″x3″x3″
B. Two pieces, each 32½″x3″x3″
C. Two pieces, each 23¾″x4″x2″
D. Two pieces, each 22¼″x9″x¾″
E. Two pieces, each 27¼″x9″x¾″
F. One piece, 69″x3″x¼″
G. One piece, 70½″x9″x¾″
H. Two pieces, each 9¼″x3″x¾″
 I. Three drawers, each: front, one piece, 19⅞″x
     3⅞″x¾″; sides, two pieces, 24⅜″x3⅞″x¾″;
     back, one piece, 18⅜″x3⅞″x¾″; bottom, one
     piece, 24″x19⅛″x¼″
J. One piece, 70½″x20″x¾″
K. Two pieces, each 68½″x4″x1″
L. Six pieces, each 26″x1″x¾″
M. One piece, 65¼″x9″x¾″

side and rear lips. Use glue and fasten with small finishing nails to hold until the glue dries.

Special care must be taken with the front legs, the tops of which have a complex shape. The special leg detail drawing shows the slope of the top surface; the triangular section which is sawed from the inside corner to provide a bearing surface for the top front 1x4; and the dado for the side. For the sake of clarity, the dado for the bottom front 1x4 is not indicated in this drawing.

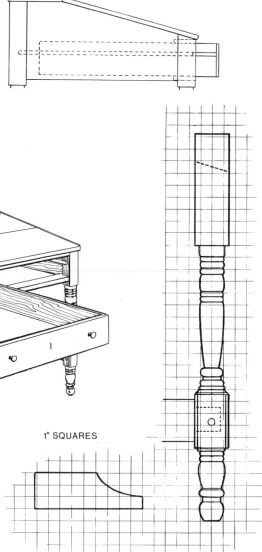

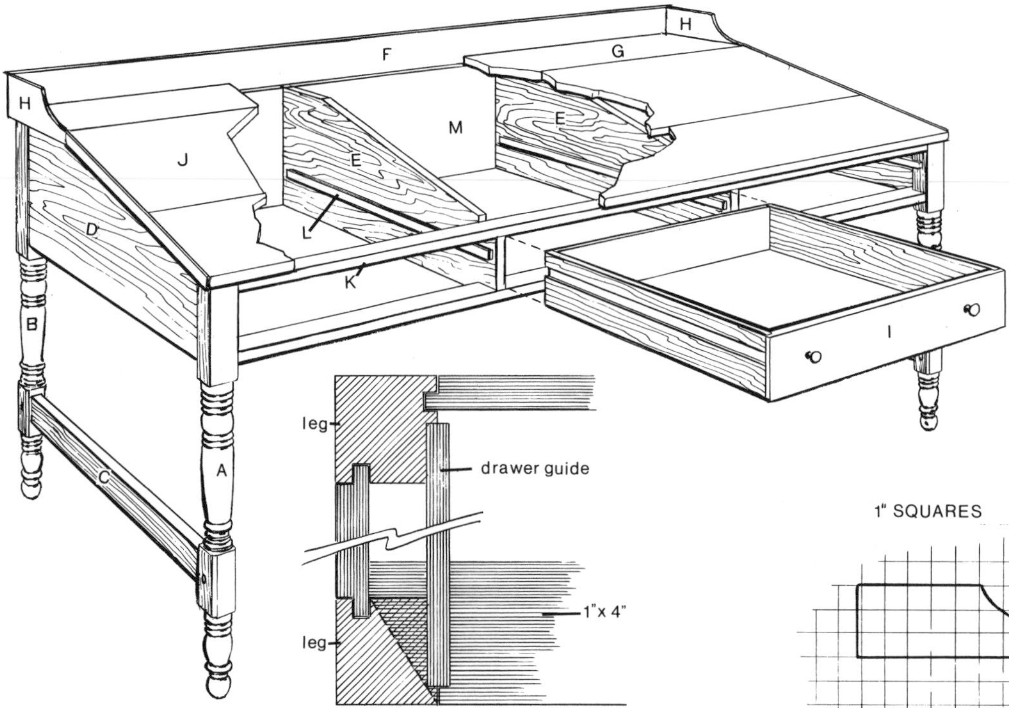

1″ SQUARES

leg

drawer guide

1″x 4″

leg

section through left side

PROJECT 43—*HUTCH-TYPE DESK*

As desks go, this model is a cut above many early American designs because its traditionally sturdy construction is kept to a straight-line appearance that fares well among any room furnishings. And do not let the photograph fool you, for the desk is compactly trim, being less than 3 feet wide at the flip-top and under 5 feet in total height. Allowing for size modifications, it would make an excellent component in a built-in series, as well as an individual accent piece.

The lighter tone or finish of the drawer faces adds to the desk's attractiveness, a feature you may want to retain for your reproduction. Accordingly, select pine, ash, maple or beech for their naturally lighter tones and cherry or walnut for the desk proper—or, simply stain any of the lighter materials to produce the same effect. You might even consider veneering in lieu of staining.

Stock is ¾ inch for the stationery top (22½x 32½), flip-top frame, drawer shelves, two-piece legs and side cross members, and beveled top-piece. Use ½ inch stock for the drawer faces, the small shelves (including upper and lower trim) and the two sides of the shelf unit. Quarter inch plywood is used for upper and lower units. Half inch stock is also used for the two inset pieces of the flip-top. Quarter inch stock is specified for the drawer sides and bottoms, the two lower, inset side panels and the overall back. Scrap stock will do for the shelf cleats and drawer guides, but use ½ inch strips for the four corner uprights within the shelf unit.

As the sketch shows, both the flip-top and desk sides are paneled, the frames being doweled and edge-glued. Assemble the two desk sides first, minus the front and rear leg halves, join the sides with the drawer shelves (after first notching the front edge corners and installing the drawer guides), stationery top and back, and then add the front and rear leg halves. Glue and nail these members.

For the shelf unit, first attach the uprights to

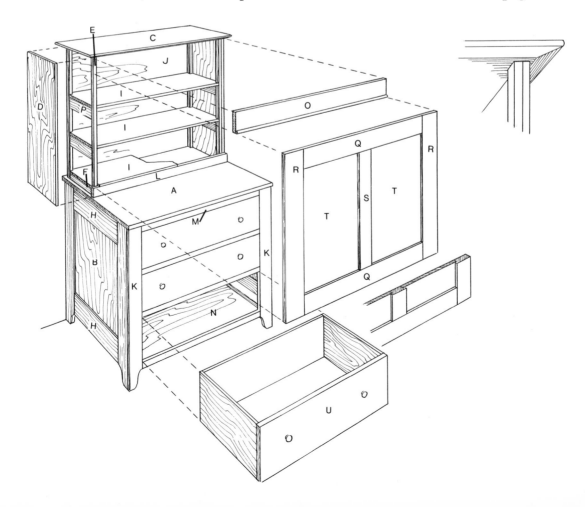

the sides, add the cleats and then join the sides with the beveled top piece and two pieces of trim. Secure the shelf unit to the desk proper through the bottom cleats and lower face trim. Add the back and slip the shelves into place.

Now, you can safely measure and cut for the flip-top, assuring a perfect fit with the shelf unit. Mortise-hinge the top and install a suitable lock.

LIST OF MATERIALS

A. One piece, 33½"x22½"x¾"
B. Two pieces, each 21½"x26¼"x½"
C. One piece, 33½"x12"x¾"
D. Two pieces, each 26½"x11"x½"
E. Four pieces, each 26½"x¾"x¾"
F. Two pieces, each 9½"x1½"x¾"
G. One piece, 26¼"x30½"x¼" (not shown)
H. Four pieces, each 15¾"x2½"x¾"
I. Three pieces, each 10¾"x30½"x¾"
J. One piece, 30½"x26½"x¼"
K. Six pieces, each 29¼"x2½"x¾"
L. One piece, 31½"x1½"x1½"
M. Eight pieces, each 28"x1½"x¾"
N. One piece, 27½"x20"x¼"
O. One piece, 31½"x3"x1½"
P. Four pieces, 9½"x1"x¾"
Q. Two pieces, each 26½"x2½"x1¼"
R. Two pieces, each 24¼"x2½"x1¼"
S. One piece, 19¼"x2½"x1¼"
T. Two pieces, 20¼"x13"x½"
U. Three drawers, each: front, one piece, 28"x 7¾"x¾"; sides, two pieces, 21"x7¾"x½"; back, one piece, 27"x7¾"x½"; bottom, one piece, 27"x20½"x½"
V. Six pieces, each 21½"x2½"x¾" (not shown)

PROJECT 44—
EARLY AMERICAN CHAIR

This chair is pictured in Project 43. While the chair is made like the others in this book, it does require lathe work to shape the legs. If you wish, decorative cuts may be made in the legs and supports to conform with the illustration. The back as detailed in the working drawing is not shaped as shown in the picture. If you shape the back, it may be cut with a curve on a band saw.

LIST OF MATERIALS

A. One piece, 16″x15″x1¼″
B. Four pieces, each 17½″x1¾″ diameter
C. Two pieces, each 12″x½″ diameter
D. One piece, 13″x½″ diameter
E. One piece, 11″x½″ diameter
F. Two pieces, each 20″x1¼″ diameter
G. One piece, 12½″x5″x1″ (or thicker piece if shaped as discussed in text)
H. Four pieces, each 14″x½″ diameter

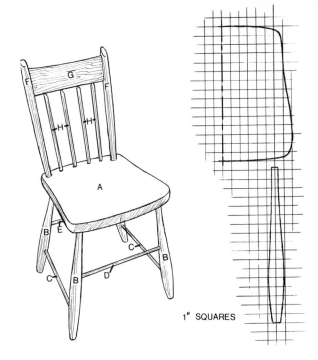

1″ SQUARES

PROJECT 45—*LADY'S COLONIAL DESK*

This unassuming, lightly-turned lady's desk is a typical product of straightforward furniture design from the days of the American colonies. We may justifiably speculate that it saw previous service as a table, and one day had sides and a back added by the local colonial handyman. Or, if originally a desk, the curious location of the small drawer suggests that at least one early American lady had a penchant for frequently using its contents, and consequently arranged to have it placed to one side for convenience while seated.

After spindle-turning the 2x2's on a lathe (reducing the stock to the cylindrical shape shown in the graph), cut eight grooves, each ¼x⅜x5, in the tops of the legs. Precut the boards for the underframe, and precut the facing underframe, as well, to accommodate the drawer size you want. Then, assemble the four legs and the four sides, using glue in the grooves. Clamp each two-leg-and-frame combination.

While the corner joints are drying, make your drawer and drawer supports (with guides) as a separate project. Butt all joints, gluing and nailing. Use the drawer opening in the table framework as a measure, being sure to provide slight play.

There are six drawer guides in all—one on each side of the drawer, and two (in the form of a groove) on each drawer support. Provide slight play here, also, so that the sliding action of the grooved guides is free.

With the drawer completed and its supports ready to be installed, cut the 18x33½ desk top. Then, cut the two sides and the decorative back, following the sketch-and-graph guide. This done, secure the back to the desk top, flush with the lower edge; then, attach the sides to the top and back.

Returning to the framework, remove all clamps. Glue and nail the drawer supports in place: first, the right one, against the sides of the front and rear leg tops; next, the left one, with the drawer held in place to assure slight play. Nail through the front and rear underframes at the point of the left support.

The final step in the assembly is to glue the top to the underframe. If you wish, nail through the top, countersink the heads, and use wood filler in the holes.

Give all surfaces a good going-over with a medium and fine sandpaper. If you want to age the piece, score and mar the surface slightly and apply dark stain with a Q-tip applicator in corners and cracks.

LIST OF MATERIALS

A. Four pieces, each 28″x2″x2″
B. Two pieces, each 26⅞″x5″x½″
C. Two pieces, each 13½″x5″x½″
D. One piece, 32½″x18″x¾″
E. Two pieces, each 18⅜″x4″x⅜″
F. One piece, 32½″x9″x⅜″
G. Two pieces, each 14½″x4″x½″
H. Six pieces, each 13¾″x1″x½″ (drawer slides —not marked)
I. One drawer: front, one piece, 8½″x3½″x¾″; sides, two pieces, 13¾″x3½″x⅜″; back, one piece, 7¾″x3½″x⅜″; bottom, one piece, 13⅜″x 7¾″x¼″

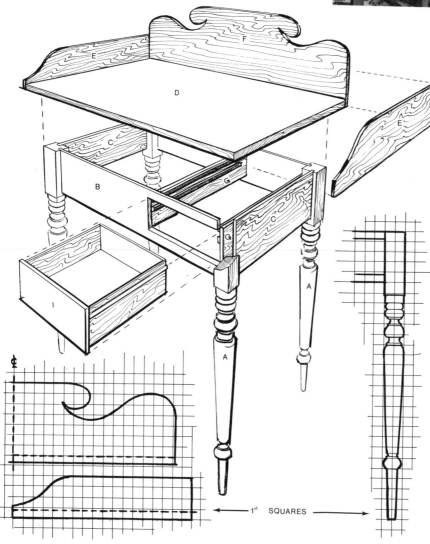

1″ SQUARES

PROJECT 46—*WRITING CADDY*

This decorative, yet practical, Victorian stationery box is of English origin, but it is not unlike those often found among the accoutrements of American Civil War officers. Construct the box itself of ½ inch plywood or pine, assembling with glue and brads. Cut ¼ inch deep dadoes in a ½ inch base for the partition section; glue in ⅛ inch box-board dividers. Glue cleats inside the box, then glue the partition assembly to its cleats. The drawer and lift-out tray are assembled as shown. Date cards can be hand-lettered. Doors are assembled with glue and brads; doors and lid are then hinged to the box. The original hardware consists of a tiny sliding bolt, at the top of the right-hand door, that catches under the closed lid, and a latch on the drawer. This latch engages the right-hand door when the left-hand door is closed. The left-hand door is then held shut by a small lock. You might enjoy rummaging through a specialty hardware store or an old curiosity shop to see what hardware you might find to approximate this, or you may improvise with small cabinet hardware.

LIST OF MATERIALS

A. Two pieces, each 10½"x11⅜"x½"
B. One piece, 11¼"x1⅜"x¾"
C. One piece, 12¼"x10½"x½"
D. One piece, 11¼"x6"x½"
E. Five pieces, each ⅛" boxboard cut to size and shape
F. One tray; front and back, 2 pieces, 11¼"x 1⅝"x⅛"; partitions, four pieces, 1⅜"x1½"x⅛"; bottom, 1 piece, 11"x1⅜"x⅛"
G. One piece, 11⅜"x11¼"x½"
H. One piece, 11¾"x2⅜"x¾"
I. Two doors: as shown in construction drawing.
J. One drawer: front, one piece, 11¼"x1½"x½"; sides, two pieces, 9½"x1¼"x½"; back, one piece, 10¾"x1¼"x½"; bottom, one piece, 10¾" x9"x¼"

cleats and ¼ round molding as needed

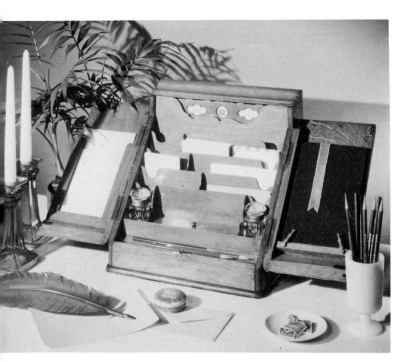

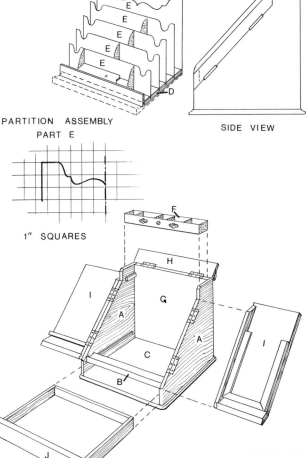

PARTITION ASSEMBLY
PART E

1" SQUARES

SIDE VIEW

PROJECT 47—

SHAKER SEWING DESK

To work at this desk, the Shaker sister would put her chair sideways at the front of the desk. The unit has plenty of handy drawer space, so that all the things she needed would be within arm's length. The box on the right side of the desk is especially interesting. Boxes of this sort were made with thin strips of wood that were boiled to make them supple, then connected with finer joints that gave them great strength. As with so many other Shaker inventions, the method was widely used for many years.

Use solid stock throughout. Start with the legs,

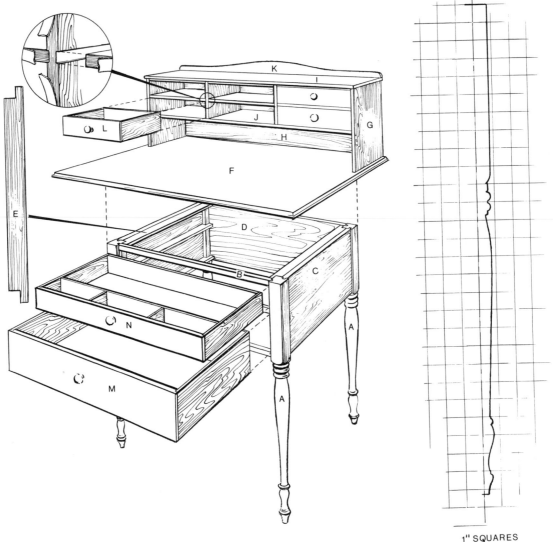

1" SQUARES

which are turned from 2x2 stock according to the graph detail, then glue them to the front drawer dividers as well as the sides and back, clamping the assembly to assure square corners. Then glue and screw on the notched drawer runners as shown. In addition to serving as runners, these pieces reinforce the back and sides. Next, fasten the one-piece work surface in place with glue and screws through the top runners, and assemble the six-drawer section that rests on it. The back and sides of this part can be rabbeted together. Use ½ inch plywood for the drawer partitions and dado them together. Hide the joints with ⅛″ inch thick facing strips of the wood you are using.

The decorative piece at the top is attached after the rest of the desk is assembled. Then fit the drawers. You may prefer to use wooden knobs instead of the porcelain ones shown.

LIST OF MATERIALS

A. Four pieces, each 27¼″x1¾″x1¾″
B. Three pieces, each 22½″x¾″x¾″
C. Two pieces, each 15½″x9½″x¾″
D. One piece, 22½″x9½″x¾″
E. Six pieces, each 16¼″x1¼″x¾″
F. One piece, 32″x22″x¾″
G. Two pieces, each 11½″x8″x½″
H. One piece, 30″x11½″x½″
 I. One piece, 31½″x9″x½″
J. Drawer partitions, cut to fit using ½″ plywood
K. Decorative strip, 1 inch at the ends, rising to 2⅛″ at the middle, and 31½″ long.
L. Six drawers, cut to fit using ¾ inch face stock.
M. One front, 21¼″x4½″x¾″; two sides, 16¾″x 4½″x½″; one back, 20″x4½″x½″
N. One front, 21¼″x2½″x¾″; two sides, 16¾″x 2½″x½″; one back, 20″x2½″x½″

⅛ inch strips to cover partition joints on top—about 126 inches of facing stock

PROJECT 48—*SEWING CABINET*

This sewing cabinet is ideal for women since it contains more than adequate storage space for pins, needles, thread, patterns and materials. And, because of its simple, sturdy lines, it could also blend in with many different decors and be used equally as well as a chest of drawers.

While there is no set way to build this project, it is recommended that you save the drawers for last. A combination of different types of joints are used to secure the various pieces of pine wood together. Many of the smaller structural members are secured using dadoes and rabbets. Some of the larger items, such as pieces E and F, are joined with simple butt joints. The four fillers (II) can be cut to size from the scraps left after piece "I" has been cut from its original stock. These fillers are optional and do not appear in the original. Nails and glue are used throughout to make the joints secure.

A peculiarity of this sewing stand is the several different sizes of drawers used—the original had no less than five different drawer sizes. For fewer headaches, we have reduced the number of drawer sizes to four. As noted on the drawing, the top two drawers (Q) go into the space indicated by the dashed lines. The same is true of the drawer designated "O" on the drawing and noted at the lower part of the drawing by a single asterisk. Also in the lower part of the drawing, the item "N" designated with two asterisks goes into the area immediately below drawer "O." The two spaces immediately below "N" receive drawer "M" noted with the three asterisks shown. Instead of the wooden drawer pulls (R), you could easily lend a distinctive note to the sewing stand by substituting porcelain. As far as finishing the unit is concerned, the original pine in this unit had a reddish orange stain.

LIST OF MATERIALS

A. Six pieces, each 25½″x2½″x¾″ (one not shown)

B. Four pieces, each 14½″x2½″x¾″

C. Four pieces, each 38″x3½″x¾″

D. Eight pieces, each 17⅛″x¾″x⅜″ (two not shown)

E. One piece, 43″x26¼″x⅜″

F. Two pieces, each 33″x18″x⅜″

G. One piece, 25½″x17⅝″x¾″

H. Eight dowels, each 2½″x⅜″ (diameter), (seven not shown)

I. Two pieces, each 17⅝″x9¼″x¾″

II. Four pieces, each cut to fit from "I" (one not shown)

J. Two pieces, each 24¾″x5½″x¾″

K. One piece, 5½″x4 1/16″x¾″

L. Two pieces, 1″ molding, each 18″ (one not shown)

M. Two drawers, each one front, 24 11/16″x7¼″x ¾″: two sides, 16⅝″x7¼″x¾″: one back, 23 3/16″x7¼″x½″: one bottom, 23 3/16″x16⅜″x¼″ (not shown)

N. One drawer, one front, 24 11/16″x7″x¾″: two sides, 16⅝″x7″x¾″: one back, 23 3/16″x7″x½″: one bottom, 23 3/16″x16⅜″x¼″ (not shown)

O. One drawer, one front, 24 11/16″x5½″x¾″: two sides, 16⅝″x5½″x¾″: one back, 23 3/16″x5½″x ½″: one bottom, 23 3/16″x16⅜″x¼″

P. Sixteen drawer slides, each 16⅝″x¾″x⅜″ (fourteen not shown)

Q. Two drawers, each, one front, 11 15/16″x 3½″x¾″: two sides, 5⅛″x3½″x½″: one back, 11 7/16″x3½″x½″: one bottom, 11 7/16″x5⅛″x¼″ (one not shown)

R. Six drawer pulls (not shown)

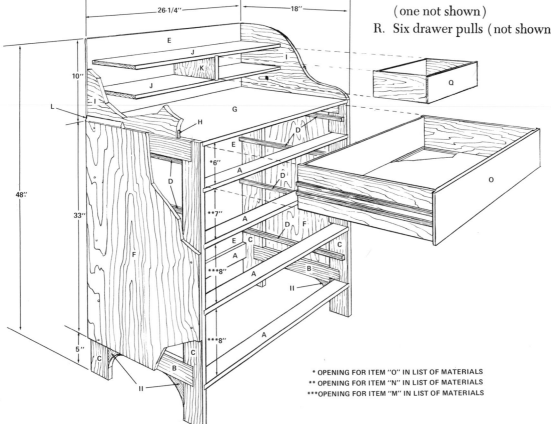
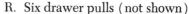

* OPENING FOR ITEM "O" IN LIST OF MATERIALS
** OPENING FOR ITEM "N" IN LIST OF MATERIALS
***OPENING FOR ITEM "M" IN LIST OF MATERIALS

PROJECT 49—*HOODED CRADLE*

Many of the colonial pieces that we see today are actually adaptations of the original design, changed to fit modern needs but retaining the colonial look. Only the colonial cradle has been immune to these changes. One reason for this is that it performs its function just as well today as it did more than 150 years ago. The cradle turned out by Early American cabinetmakers was just as attractive as it was functional, and today it has the added appeal of romantic quaintness. There also seems to be a special sense of security in entrusting the family's precious bundle to a bed that reflects our Puritan heritage. It is as if the honest, humble strength of our nation's founders is summoned to stand guard while the new citizen sleeps.

These plans will provide a replica of a cradle from a site which was in itself a cradle of the American Revolution—Lexington, Massachusetts. The butt-joint construction is simple and requires only the usual hand tools.

Make full-size patterns of the front, cornice and side-apron scrolls, and of the rockers. Trace these patterns on 1 inch white knotty pine stock (actual thickness ¾ inch) and cut to shape with a sabre saw or jig saw. A piece 10½″x17″ is large enough for the front, but you will have to edge-join (with dowels) several pieces to form the sides, as indicated in the sketch. The ends of these pieces are canted about 9 degrees outside the vertical so the bottom edges have to be beveled correspondingly. With brads, temporarily assemble front, sides and cornice, and take the exact measurements for the back member. The pattern for the top edge will be identical to that of the cornice. Since all edges of the back panel are hidden, it may be cut from ¾ inch plywood.

Cut the three rectangles for the "roof" of the hood from stock ½ inch thick, and bevel their long edges. These pieces set flush with the outside faces of the upright members. Apply glue to all butting surfaces and assemble the five upright members with screws. Countersink the heads and peg with dowels. This provides both sturdy construction and a hand-crafted charm.

Keep in mind that you are making an heirloom.

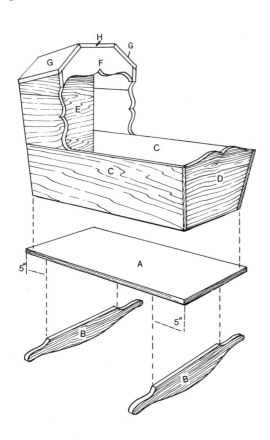

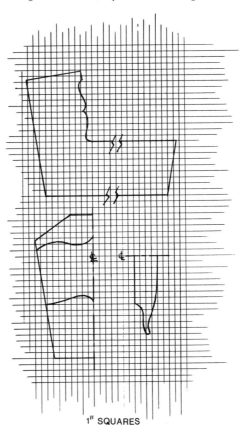

1″ SQUARES

A generous patina of nostalgia is bound to accrue as the original occupant matures and, in turn, has need of a cradle for the latest addition to his or her own family. In the interim, the cradle is likely to be pressed into service as a toy box, so build sturdily for generations of hard use.

The three roof units are secured with glue and finishing nails. Set the heads and cover with wood putty. Drive screws down through the bottom to secure the rockers and up through the bottom to join this unit to the uprights.

Round all edges with a cornering tool, file or coarse sandpaper. Finish as desired.

LIST OF MATERIALS

A. One piece, 32″x16″x¾″
B. Two pieces, each 26″x4″x¾″
C. Two pieces, each 36″x21″x¾″
D. One piece, 10½″x16½″x¾″
E. One piece, 23⅞″x20″x¾″
F. One piece, 5⅞″x20″x¾″
G. Two pieces, each 6″x9½″x¾″
H. One piece, 4″x9½″x¾″

PROJECT 50—*CHILD'S ROCKER*

Bench time in putting any or all of these projects together is kept to a minimum, as the sketches tell the complete story, including the List of Materials. The captivating little rocker, only 27 inches high, is a quickie to construct, following the inch-square graph accompanying the sketch. The dotted lines in the primary sketch show how a large board cleat is used to join the tail of the rocker to the basic panel (also serving as a support for the seat). Additionally, the seat back and sides are strengthened with the corner wedges.

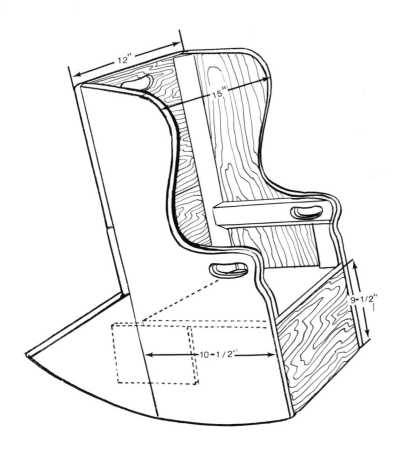

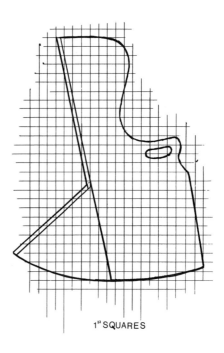

1" SQUARES

PROJECT 51—*CHILD'S DESK*

This little desk is quite interesting. The drawer you see in front is not a drawer at all, but a section of skirting with a china knob attached to it. On the left side there is a drawer for writing paper and the like that runs the full length of the piece. Also on the left side, inside the desk, there is a tray for pens and pencils. Most interesting feature of all is the little drawer on the right side. This was for holding a bottle of ink; the drawer could be pulled out to its full length without falling, holding the bottle securely and within easy reach.

We have retained, within fractions of an inch, the original dimensions of the piece. They are small, so the use of solid stock is practicable. The original is pine but you can, of course, select the stock you like best. Think of the piece as being basically a table, and you will be able to visualize construction better.

The table section of the piece is built first with the legs, tapered on the insides only, attached to the skirting with their fronts flush as shown. The top of the table is a piece of ¼ inch plywood. The front, back and right side are dadoed on the inside to accept the desk bottom, then these and the other side are assembled with dovetails. The assembly is then attached to the table top. If you have never used dovetails for joinery, this is a good place to start. They enhance the looks of the piece considerably, yet will not involve an inordinate amount of time to make. Of course, you could simply butt the sections together. Then, add the molding strips around the edges of the table top.

Cut out the section for the ink bottle drawer next, and fit the drawer. As shown in the detail, this drawer has one extra long side slotted so it rides on a fixed piece attached to the back of the piece. This arrangement lets you pull this little drawer all the way out without fear of its falling out. Attach the pen tray to the side next, then fit the drawer, which simply fits into the piece and does not require rails. Finally, hinge the lid of the desk to the back. As you can see in the sketch, this is composed of individual boards. It can be assembled by tongue and grooves or edge-glued together. As far as a finish goes, you will want to consider using something durable if the piece is going to be used by a child (see Section III).

LIST OF MATERIALS

A. Four pieces, each 21¾"x1⅛"x1⅛" (tapered to ¾" square at the bottom)

B. Two pieces, each 11¾"x3⅛"x¾"

C. One piece, 21"x13"x¼"

D. One desk unit: one front, 21"x4½"x¾"; one back, 21"x6"x¾"; left side, 13"x3¾" (at back end) x2½" (at front end) x¾"; right side, 13"x6" (at back end) x4½" (at front end) x¾"

E. One piece, 20½"x12"x½"

F. One ink bottle drawer: short side 3¼"x2"x¼"; long side, 7"x3"x¼"; front, 2¾"x2"x¼"; face, 3¼"x2½"x¼"

G. Piece of molding sized to suit

H. One drawer, size to fit

I. One piece, 21¾"x13¾"x½"

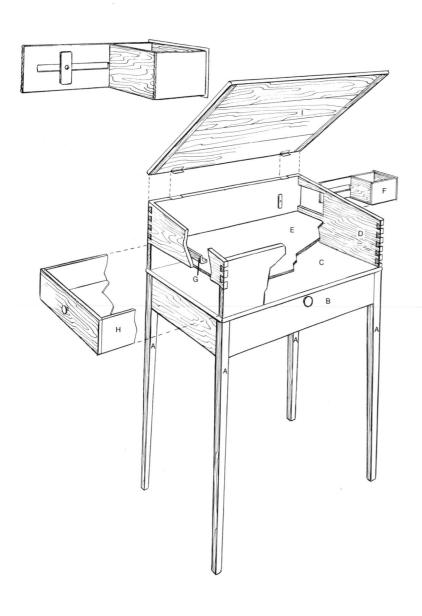

PROJECT 52—*PENNSYLVANIA DUTCH TOWEL RACK*

As noted in this book, early American furniture is not confined solely to New England. Many unique and respectably aged pieces are to be found in Pennsylvania too, as evidenced by the unusual Pennsylvania Dutch towel rack shown here. Few early American pieces can be so easily reproduced as this one or, when finished, can blend so gracefully into almost any early American background. Both useful and ornamental, this towel rack will readily brighten any otherwise bleak corner and will certainly display to best advantage some of the family's finest linen.

To duplicate it, cut all pieces to size from clear pine. The pattern for the traditional heart design of the end pieces must be enlarged to full scale and transferred to 1x10 inch stock. Cut out with a scroll or coping saw (by hand) or with a jig, band or sabre saw (if using power equipment).

Attach all cross pieces with counterset flathead screws put through the ends, two screws into each end of the 1x2 inch pieces. Neater and firmer joints can be created by cutting ¼ inch deep recesses for these crosspieces with a sharp chisel and gluing them in place before inserting screws.

Round exposed edges of all parts irregularly with a wood rasp, then sand smooth. Apply desired finish.

LIST OF MATERIALS
A. Two pieces, each 28″x10″x1″
B. Two pieces, each 24″x2″x1″
C. Four pieces, each 24″x1″x1″

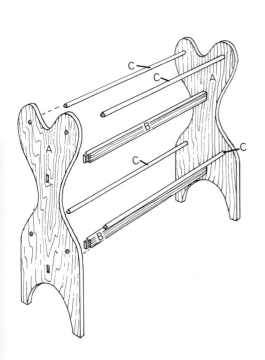

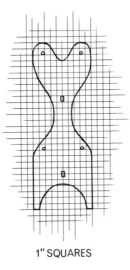

1″ SQUARES

PROJECT 53—*CANDLE STAND*

A candle can give a room a softly elegant charm—if the occasion is not a power blackout. And even if you do not use candles often enough to justify building this Shaker candle stand, you could still find wide use for it as an occasional table that could blend in easily with early American or colonial decors. The original of this candle stand, used in the Sabbathday Lake Shaker Community in Maine, differs from most of the ones you would find later because of its stick or peg legs and its unusual rectangular top. But despite the fact that the legs are tapered, the actual building of the candle stand is quite easy. It is so easy that you may be able to do it in only a few hours—assuming, of course, that you have the necessary lathe on which to turn the tapered legs (B) and the central column (A).

No nails were used in building this candle stand which with the exception of the maple top (D) is made from pine. Piece C has a 3 inch hole drilled through its center. It is suggested the top (D) be joined to piece C using four screws and glue before piece A is attached as shown in detail 3. The central column (A) is joined to piece C with glue.

After the three legs are turned using the pattern in detail 1, they are cut off at 45 degree angles as indicated. The top dotted line in detail 1 shows the angle of the leg holes in piece A shown in detail 2. Next, holes are drilled in piece A at a 45 degree angle to receive the three legs which are attached with glue.

Although the way you finish this piece is optional, the original piece had a red stain.

LIST OF MATERIALS
A. One piece, 19¾″x3″ diameter
B. Three pieces, each 15″x1″ diameter
C. One piece, 6″x6″x2″
D. One piece, 20″x14½″x1″

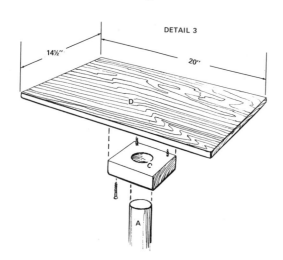

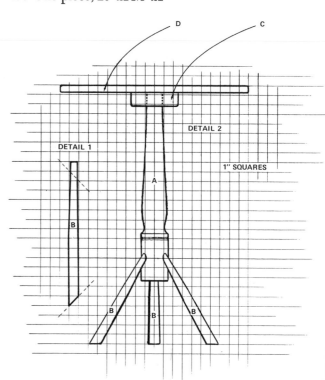

PROJECT 54—*CURIO SHELF*

This typically colonial background piece will enliven any early American setting with its own mellow charm, and then go further by offering display space for your valued bric-à-brac.

The unit lends itself to two methods of construction. If you have simple hand tools, it can be put together with a saw, hammer, nail set and glue, and the scroll work can be handled with a scroll or jig saw. More intricate joining can be accomplished with a full array of power tools. Choose the method that pleases you best. Both types of joints are shown.

Cut the top, bottom and drawer top equal in size and bevel one edge of each on front and ends. Cut five identical pieces for shelves and use the other two as top and bottom inserts. Then cut sides. The ornamental scroll is attached to the top insert. The back is made by joining random pieces of beveled pine, tongue-and-grooved stock. Note that in making shelves and inserts these pieces will be somewhat longer if they are inset in dadoes in the sides.

Drawers may be simple butt-joined boxes, or the more intricate joining technique may be followed if you have power tools.

LIST OF MATERIALS

A. Two pieces, each 24¾"x3¾"x⅜"
B. Two pieces, each 20½"x4¼"x¾"
C. One piece, 20½"x4¼"x⅜"
D. Five pieces, each 18⁵⁄₁₆"x3"x⅜"
E. One piece, 24¾"x18⅜"x¾"
F. Two pieces, each 2⅝"x3¾"x⅜"
G. One piece, 19"x¾"x⅜"
H. Two drawers, each 4⅝"x3¼"x2½" (not shown)
I. One drawer, 8"x3¼"x2½" (not shown)
J. One piece, 2⅝"x18"x¼"
K. Two pieces, each 2⅝"x3¼"x⅜"
L. Three drawer knobs, each ½" diameter (not shown)

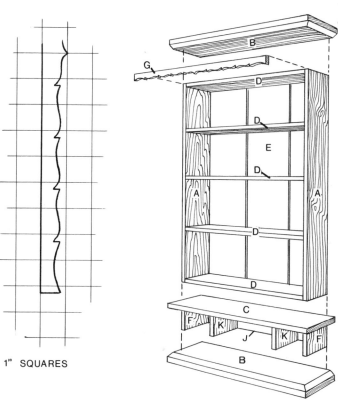

1" SQUARES

PROJECT 55—*LETTER RACK*

Perhaps you have caught a glimpse of and secretly admired one of those antique cabinets or racks that occasionally appear on the walls of the home of your favorite television personalities. With a little effort you can have one of your own. Here is a copy of an antique letter rack that has grace and charm enough to adorn any stage setting or home. Hang it in the entrance hall or foyer for a handy place to put those important letters. The three drawers serve as an ideal location for stamps, keys or other small articles.

With the exception of the slotted upright for displaying the mail, the entire rack may be constructed of lumber selected from the sides of apple or pear shipping boxes. You can use maple, pine or birch.

Here is the construction technique step-by-step:

1. Trace pattern A on back piece and cut to shape with coping saw.

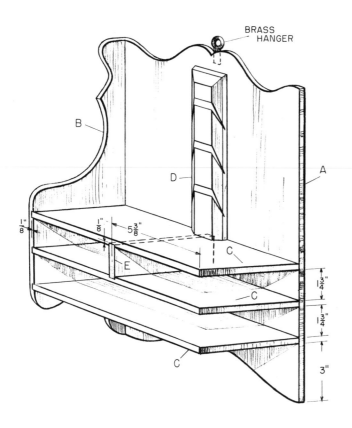

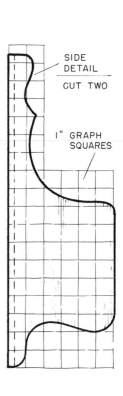

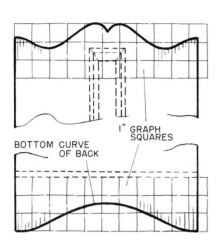

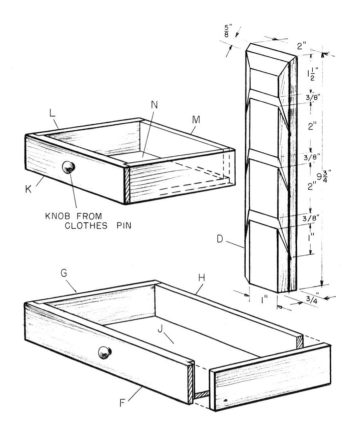

I" GRAPH
SQUARES

BOTTOM CURVE
OF BACK

KNOB FROM
CLOTHES PIN

2. Trace pattern B on both side pieces "B" and cut to shape.

3. Cut three dadoes or grooves into each side (see sketch) to accommodate shelves "C." Cut with back saw to a depth of ⅛ inch and remove excess with chisel.

4. Cut a dado ⅛ inch deep and ⁵⁄₁₆ inch wide in the underside of the top shelf and the upper surface of the center shelf (see sketch) to provide for the divider "E."

5. Bevel the edges of the rack "D" with a plane; then cut slots for the letter with a back saw (see detail).

6. Cut rabbets along outside edge of drawer faces "F" and "K" with a back saw so that drawer sides fit flush. Rabbet is ¼ inch wide and ⅛ inch deep.

LIST OF MATERIALS

A. One piece, 17½"x10½"x⁵⁄₁₆"

B. Two pieces, each 17½"x6¹⁄₁₆"x⁵⁄₁₆"

C. Three pieces, each 10¾"x5¾"x⁵⁄₁₆"

D. One piece, 9¾"x2"x¾"

E. One piece, 5¾"x2"x⁵⁄₁₆"

F. One piece, 10⅜"x1¹¹⁄₁₆"x⁵⁄₁₆"

G. Two pieces, each 5½"x1¹¹⁄₁₆"x¼"

H. One piece, 9⅞"x1⁷⁄₁₆"x¼"

J. One piece, 9¾"x5⅝"x¼"

K. Two pieces, each 5"x1¹¹⁄₁₆"x⁵⁄₁₆"

L. Four pieces, each 5½"x1¹¹⁄₁₆"x¼"

M. Two pieces, each 4½"x1⁷⁄₁₆"x¼"

N. Two pieces, each 4½"x5⅝"x¼"

PROJECT 56—*HANGING CUPBOARD*

Spice and herb boxes were a necessity in the early American kitchen, and often were considered almost a part of a young lady's dowry. The doors on this one are beveled panels in a tongue and groove assembly.

This spice chest is built of 1x8 pine boards, with shelves ripped to a width of 7 inches. The top shelf is 8⅜ inches wide. Door frames are 1x3 inch pieces grooved to receive ¼ inch plywood panels. Grooves are cut with a dado blade or kerfed on a table saw. The doors are rabbeted to overlap and are recessed into a rabbet on the top shelf as shown.

LIST OF MATERIALS

A. One piece, 18″x6¼″x¾″
B. Two pieces, each 20″x7⅝″x¾″
C. Two pieces, each 18″x7″x¾″
D. Two doors, each: frame sides, two pieces, each 19¼″x3″x1″; top and bottom, each, 5¾″x3″x 1″; panel, 14¼″x5¾″x¼″
E. One piece, ¾″ molding cut to fit
F. Two pieces, ¾″ molding cut to fit
G. One piece, 18″x1½″x¾″
H. One piece, 19″¾x8⅜″x¾″
I. Two pieces, each 6⅞″x3½″x¾″
J. One piece, 18″x6¼″x¾″
K. One piece, 20″x18″x½″

BACK
SCROLL DIAGRAM
1" SQUARES

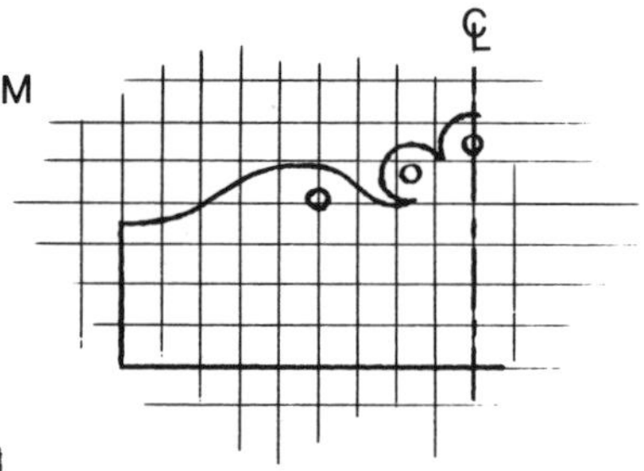

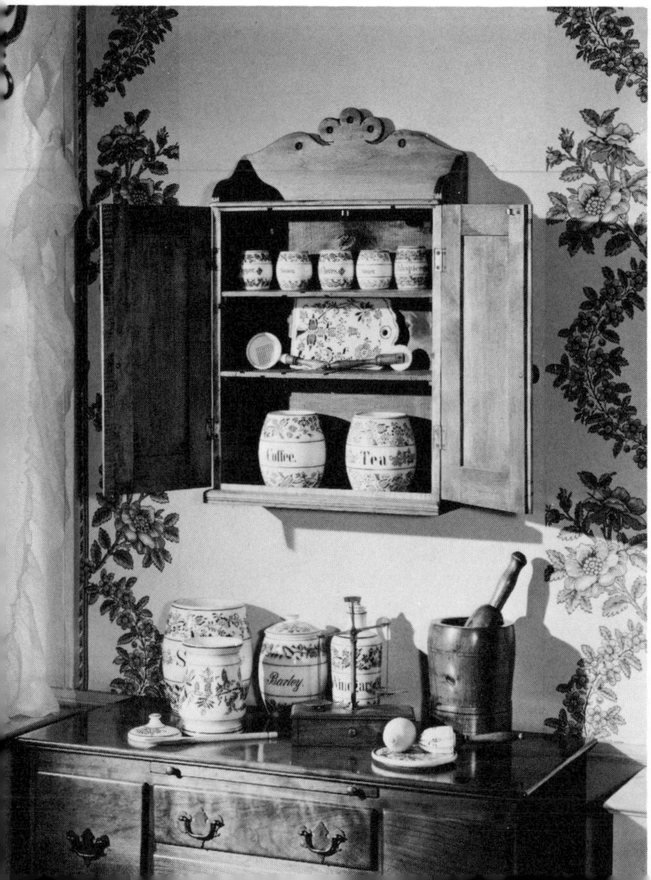

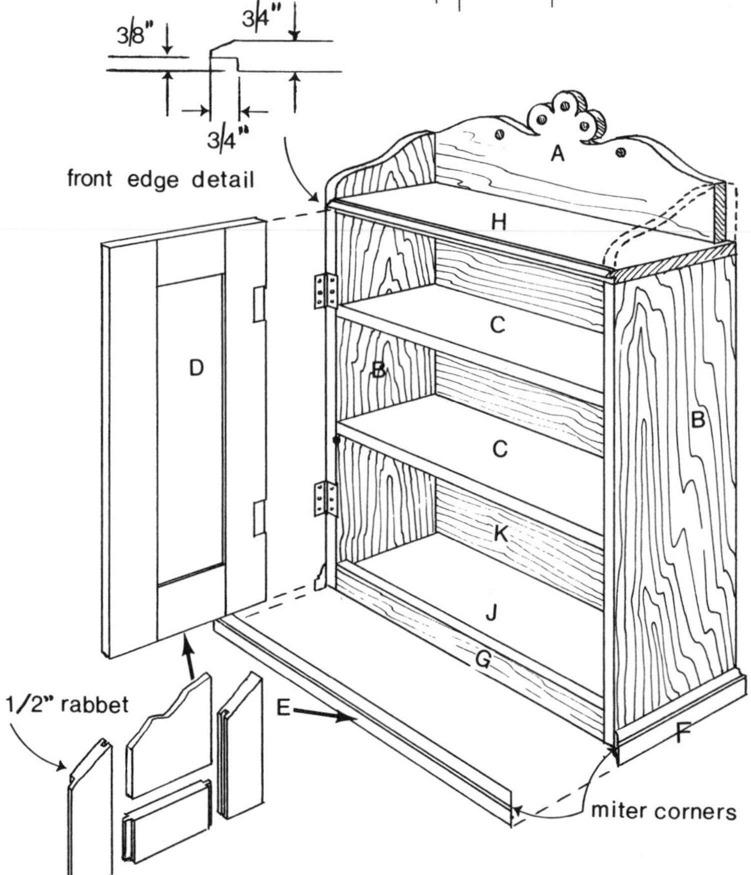

PROJECT 57—*SHAKER WOOD BOX*

There is something warm and wonderful about having an old wood box around, especially in the holiday season. It seems to fit into the spirit of things perfectly.

For the Shakers, who heated their buildings with fireplaces and stoves, a nice handy wood box was essential. There were many varieties, large and small. Some had drawers for kindling, some doors to completely close the box for neatness, and others were partitioned inside so the logs could be stacked neatly, utilizing all available space. This box has an uncommon feature: a removable towel rack set into sockets in its top. The box was undoubtedly positioned between a dry sink and stove; but if it had to be placed in a very small space elsewhere, it was a simple matter to remove the rack. The dust pan and brush hanging on the side are also Shaker made. They were handy in keeping the hearth clear of ashes.

You can build this piece easily following the drawing. You will note that all edges of the box opening are chamfered, to prevent splintering when wood was dumped in.

The original is pine stained a reddish color. You can also use pine boards, staining the piece burnt sienna with a touch of lamp black to simulate aging.

LIST OF MATERIALS

A. One piece, 28½"x11"x¾", bottom, not shown
B. Two pieces, each 36"x12"x¾"
C. One piece, 30"x14"x¾"
D. One back piece, random-width boards, each ¾" thick
E. One piece, 30"x8"x¾"
F. One towel rack, two upright each 15"x1½"x1"
Two crosspieces, each 18"x1"x1"; dowels as needed

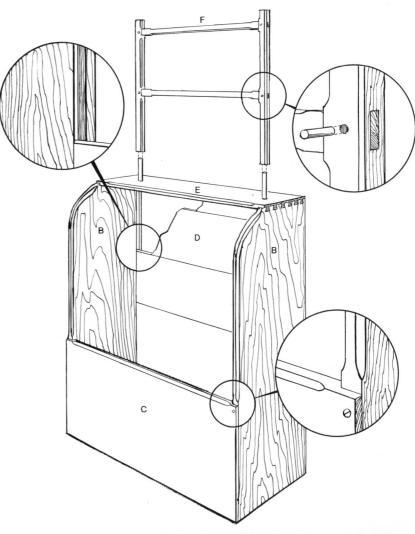

PROJECT 58—*BLACKSMITH BOX*

This truly colonial piece is almost extinct. Quite rare, and hard to find in its original state, it can still be reproduced quite easily. And reproduced, it will serve admirably as a magazine rack, as a catchall, or as a knickknack stand beside your favorite chair. Our authentic original was salvaged long ago and ornamented with an intriguing Pennsylvania Dutch design. You may omit this detail or, if you prefer, substitute an inexpensive floral decal after finishing.

Cut all pieces to size, then join the sides to the ends. Use counterset wood screws and cover the screw heads with wood plugs glued into holes. (See detail A.) Next insert the center shelf, holding it in place with similar screws. Add the trim strips which are attached with glue and brads.

Attach the top inserts to the top with glue, and

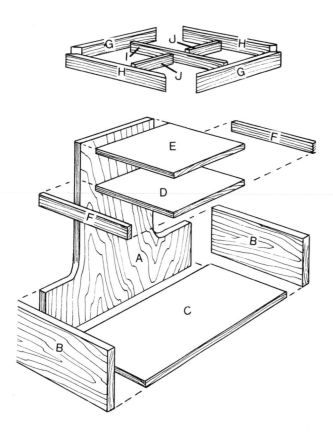

brads inserted from underneath the top. Then attach the top to the sides with finishing nails. Miter the trim strips and attach with glue and brads. Use a wood rasp to round all curves and lightly round sharp edges irregularly with this tool. Follow with a light sanding to produce the aged, colonial look. Apply antique finish desired. If you apply a decal, give it a coat of thin low-luster varnish, then wax the entire piece with paste wax in two coats.

LIST OF MATERIALS

A. Two pieces, each 15½"x16"x¾"
B. Two pieces, each 11"x4½"x¾"
C. One piece, 15½"x9½"x¾"
D. One piece, 8"x9½"x¾"
E. One piece, 8"x11"x¾"
F. Two pieces, each 1½"x11"x⅜"
G. Two pieces, each 1¾"x8¾"x⅜"
H. Two pieces, each 1¾"x11¾"x⅜"
I. One piece, 11"x1"x⅜"
J. Two pieces, each 3⁵⁄₁₆"x1"x⅜"

PROJECT 59—*SPICE BOX*

Here is an antique hanging cabinet that may be employed in various ways and several different rooms of your home. In your kitchen it may serve its original purpose for spice storage. In the sewing room it is a storage place for buttons, thread, bindings. In your shop it may serve as tackle box, or storehouse for nails and screws and washers.

When used ornamentally, the open center may be an advantage. On a papered wall, the paper exposed in the center becomes a framed picture. With a mirror behind it, the cabinet may be a frame for the mirror, or the glass may reflect some object placed on the shelf, such as a ceramic item or a small flower vase.

Base should be ½ inch material and the drawer fronts 5⁄16 inch stock. The remainder may be made up of ¼ inch lumber, except the ⅛ inch back piece. Select pieces with good grain. Use a back saw to cut square ends and a coping saw for the curved lines unless you have power tools. Make all joints butt joints with glue and brads.

Assemble from the bottom up. Make the base, add the lower drawer separator, then the crosspiece over the lower drawers, then the sides. Add the two inner uprights, the top shelf and the back piece by which the cabinet is hung on the wall. Finally, add the drawer dividers.

Drawers are then made to a loose fit. While a rabbeted edge of the drawer fronts is illustrated, to give greater strength, butt joints well glued and bradded may be substituted. In this case, the drawer front covers the end grain of the drawer sides. Knobs are cut from wood clothespins and glued into drilled holes. Add the ⅛ inch back to prevent drawers from pushing through. Then round all sharp edges slightly with a rasp or sandpaper to provide the antique look.

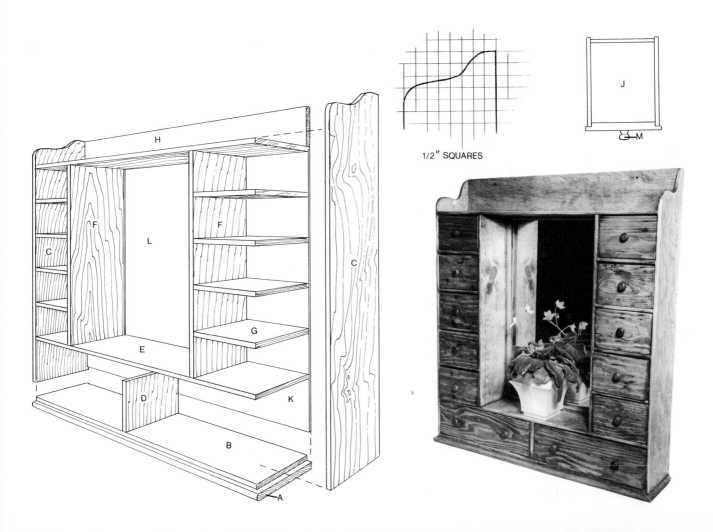

1/2" SQUARES

LIST OF MATERIALS

A. One piece, 21¼″x4⅜″x½″
B. One piece, 20″x3⅞″x¼″
C. Two pieces, each 22¾″x4″x¼″
D. One piece, 3⅞″x3¹⁄₁₆″x¼″
E. Two pieces, each 20″x4″x¼″
F. Two pieces, 16″x4″x¼″
G. Eight pieces, each 4½″x3⅞″x¼″
H. One piece, 20″x3″x¼″
I. Two drawers, each: fronts, one piece, 9¾″x3″x⁵⁄₁₆″; sides, two pieces, 3¾″x3″x¼″; backs, one piece, 9⅛″x2¾″x¼″; bottom, one piece, 9⅛″x3¼″x¼″ (not shown)
J. Ten drawers, each: fronts, one piece, 4⅜″x3″x⁵⁄₁₆″; sides, two pieces, 3¾″x3″x¼″; backs, one piece, 2¾″x2¾″x¼″; bottom, one piece, 3¾″x3¼″x¼″
K. One piece, 20″x20″x⅛″ (hardboard)
L. Mirror
M. Fourteen clothespins (knobs)

PROJECT 60—*DOUGH BOX*

Home-baked bread was a staple of the diet in early American times. It was, in fact, almost the only way that families could have bread for there was no supermarket "right around the corner" then. No account of life in those days was complete without a description of the once-or-twice-weekly ritual of bread-baking. The warm, bustling kitchen was the center of activity. While the others busied themselves with different tasks, the woman of the family had her own chore—she would mix and knead a large wad of dough. Then, when this was done, the dough had to rise before it could be baked, so she put it aside in a place that had been made for that very purpose—the dough box. Today, a dough box is rarely used in this way. If you are lucky enough to find one in an antique shop, or at a country auction, you will use it for an occasional table or even install a record player in it, under the hinged lid.

Duplicating the attractive version pictured here is a challenge. It can be done in either of two ways. Power tools are faster. You will use a table saw, a wood-turning lathe and a shaper. Or, if you want to have the interesting experience of duplicating the methods as well as the product of the old-time craftsmen, make the entire piece with hand tools alone. Besides the usual saw and hammer and such, you will also require a spokeshave and a combination plane. The spokeshave—sometimes called a draw knife—makes the taper on the legs. The combination plane makes it possible to cut a molding bead into the edge of the top and the piece right above the legs. Both tools are basically the same as those used so long ago, although parts that were made of wood are now steel and perhaps the shape has changed a bit, also.

The frame between the legs and box is a good place to start construction. Cut dado grooves in 2x2 stock ½ inch wide and ⅜ inch deep on two adjacent faces. Saw the 2x2 into four pieces for the corners. Next, cut bevels on one end of each block, as in the detailed leg drawing. Cut frame sides and ends of ½x2½ inch stock; the angle cut into the ends must match that of the corner pieces. Insert sides and ends into the grooves in the blocks, first coating all meeting surfaces with wood glue. You do not need a clamp to hold the assembly while it dries. Instead, wrap a strong cord tightly around the perimeter of the frame.

Shaping the legs calls for the use of the spoke shave. Cut a ½ inch deep V-groove in a length of 2 inch dowel all around the leg, 1 inch from its end. Next, with the spokeshave, "peel" the wood off the leg little by little, working from the top toward the groove. Keep turning the leg, shaving gradually and evenly, until it tapers smoothly from its full diameter to only 1 inch at the groove. After four legs have been made, drill ½ inch holes in the leg tops and the bottom of each corner block. Glue ½ inch dowels into the matching holes to connect legs to blocks.

The top piece is made from 1x12 inch stock. Cut it to length. Setting the adjustable blades of the combination plane to a pleasing pattern, use the tool to shape the edges of the board into the curves and beads of a handsome molding. Remember that the fancier the cut, the harder the job. Keep it simple. In fact, if this tool is not available to you, the molded edge can be eliminated entirely and it can be rounded off with a rasp, instead. Fasten this piece to the leg assembly with countersunk 2 inch flathead screws and glue.

Building the dough box itself is the next step. All stock used here is 1x12″. Cut sides and ends and fasten together with countersunk finishing nails and glue. Plane a slight angle into the top and bottom edges so that they parallel the top of the leg assembly. Next, cut the bottom to the proper length but rip it about ¼ inch wider than needed. Plane the sides of this board to match the angle of the sides of the dough box. Take off only slim shavings at a time, testing carefully for fit as you proceed. When the right shape and dimension are reached, coat edges with glue and secure with finishing nails.

The lids are made from *one* piece of ¾ inch plywood, placed so that the grain on the top runs with the long dimension of the table. Shape the edges and mortise for the butt hinges. Fasten to hinges and to the box, making sure it opens and closes freely. Then remove it and cut it in half, making it into two separate lids. By doing this, you are assured of the lids' opening and closing without interfering with each other. Having completed the box, fasten it with glue and screws driven up through the top of the leg assembly into the bottom of the box.

To complete, sand all surfaces smooth and finish with stain, varnish or wax to suit.

LIST OF MATERIALS

A. Two pieces, each 17¾″x14″x¾″
B. Two pieces, each 24¾″x12″x¾″
C. Two pieces, each 13¾″x12″x¾″
D. One piece, 19⅛″x8¼″x¾″
E. One piece, 11⅝″x20⅝″x1″
F. Two pieces, each 17⅜″x2½″x½″
G. Two pieces, each 8⅜″x2½″x½″
H. Four pieces, each 3″x2″x2″
I. Four pieces, each 12⅛″x2″ diameter

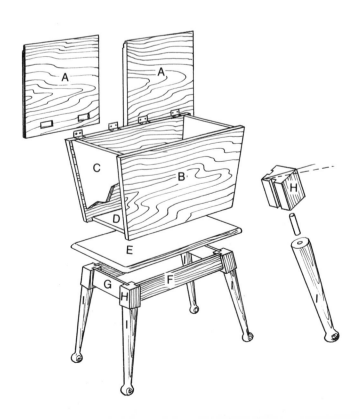

PROJECT 61—*FLOUR BOX*

During early colonial times, the general store was the gathering place of the entire community. Gossip was exchanged when trade was slow. And commodities were scooped out of boxes such as the one shown here, weighed and sold. Since shipment of flour, sugar, cornmeal, salt and other drystores was made in large bags, they were then transferred in the store to boxes of this type for easy dispensing. And, of course, the boxes were most often made by the storekeeper himself. For added attraction, the fronts of the boxes were ornamented—in this case with stenciled patterns.

To build, cut out all pieces to size and with the exception of the sides of the box lid, round all outer edges irregularly, using a rasp or medium sandpaper. Attach cleats to sides, back and front equal distance from the bottom of legs. Use 1¼ inch flathead screws to attach the cleats

from the inside. Join the sides to the back, then add the front. These joints may be made with counterset flathead screws, or counterset finishing nails. If you cut the bottom to a snug fit, it may be rested on the cleats without further attachment and can be removed at will.

Attach the fixed top, and the two side strips with counterset finishing nails. Then hinge on the lid, using brass hinges. These are available in colonial design at your hardware store.

Sand the cabinet, apply desired finish. If you want a design either stencil one on (or paint it if you are artistically inclined), or decals may be used. Paste wax (white) is then applied in several coats and may be put on directly over the designs. While this flour box is employed as a fireside wood box, yours may serve as a toy box for children, as shoe and umbrella stand in a hall-

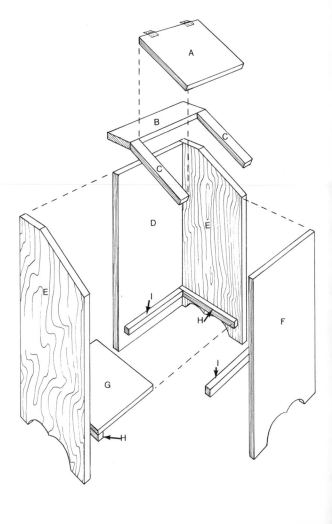

way. Or—if you do a lot of baking—as a flour box.

LIST OF MATERIALS
A. One piece, 15½″x15½″x¾″
B. One piece, 18″x4″x¾″
C. Two pieces, each 15½″x1¼″x¾″
D. One piece, 18″x37″x¾″
E. Two pieces, each 37″x17″x¾″
F. One piece, 15½″x32″x¾″
G. One piece, 15½″x15½″x¾″
H. Two pieces, each 15½″x1″x1″
I. Two pieces, each 13½″x1″x1″

PROJECT 62—*FEED BIN*

This feed bin lends itself to all sorts of storage uses around the home (the length of the bin may be altered to suit your purpose). One inch stock lumber is used throughout.

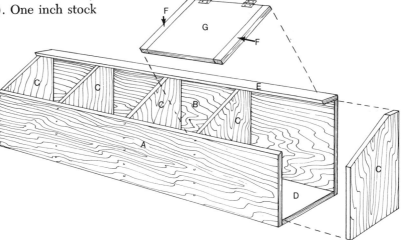

LIST OF MATERIALS
A. One piece, 56″x7⅞″x1″
B. One piece, 56″x11⅝″x1″
C. Five pieces, each 10⅞″x7⅝″x1″
D. One piece, 56″x7⅝″x1″
E. One piece, 56″x1⅝″x1″
F. Eight pieces, each 9⅝″x2″x1″
G. Four pieces, each 9⅝″x12″x1″

PROJECT 63—
CATWALK PLATE RACK

Ever since the earliest days of the country, racks of this type have been used to display the family's prized chinaware—ironstone, willow ware and other such pieces—which rarely found their way into common, everyday use. The passage of time has not lessened the pride taken in showing off one's prized possessions, and this lovely old colonial plate rack still serves the purpose as ably as ever and, in addition, is an admirable display piece in itself.

The construction is amazingly simple. Cut the various pieces to size. The patterns on the sides and on the bottom cup-rack brace can be cut by hand with a jig or a coping saw, although any

power saw suited to curve cutting will do. Round exposed edges with a wood rasp to simulate the colonial appearance, then sand smooth. A router, dado plane or power saw can be used to cut the V-shaped beads in the shelves which hold the plates upright.

Join the shelves to the sides with 10d finishing nails and wood glue, then counterset the nails. Drill peg holes in bottom brace with ½ inch bit and square them with a rasp or sharp chisel, or, if you prefer, drill the holes ⅜ inch diameter and then round the ends of the square peg stock. Attach bottom brace in same way shelves were attached and insert pegs with glue. Fill all nail holes with wood putty.

The piece illustrated was finished with antique stain and two coats of paste wax. Attach hardware brackets at upper ends of sides and hang on the wall with 60-pound picture hangers.

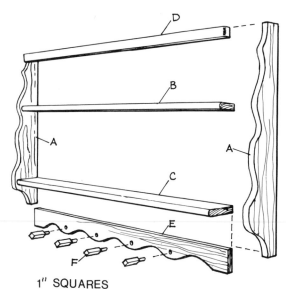

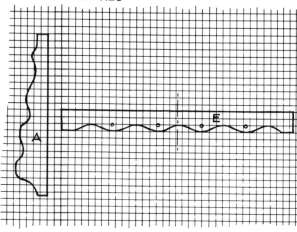

1" SQUARES

LIST OF MATERIALS
A. Two pieces, each 23½"x4¾"x1"
B. One piece, 34½"x3½"x1"
C. One piece, 34½"x4½"x1"
D. One piece, 36"x1¼"x1"
E. One piece, 34½"x3"x1"
F. Four pieces, each 2¾"x½"x½"
Picture hangers as needed.

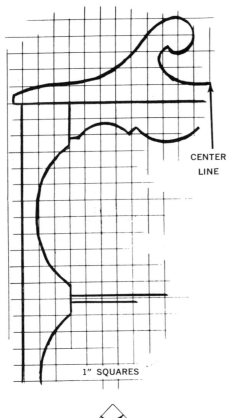

CENTER
LINE

1" SQUARES

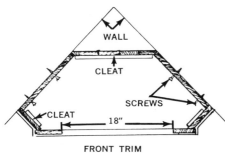

WALL

CLEAT

SCREWS

CLEAT

18"

FRONT TRIM

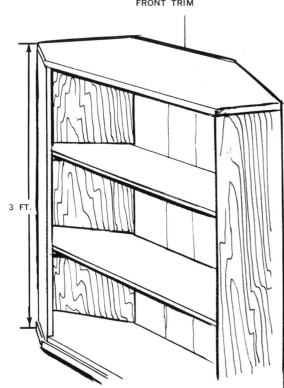

3 FT.

PROJECT 64—
CORNER SHELF

What makes this 2x3 foot early American type corner shelf especially practical for display of small articles is the absence of the usual V'ed back, its own alternative a flat-back explained in the down-view sketch. As a matter of fact, this little sketch sums up very nearly all of the simple construction steps.

Settle for ¼ or ½-inch stock throughout—well-seasoned beech, pine, maple or cherry (even some ash, if you can find any). Put together the right-angled sides first, fabricating two L's (only the short bars of the L's will show), and then nail the top to the ends of the sides. But for the bottom, nail through the sides into that shelf's edges. Random-width boards for the back are nailed and glued to the top and bottom, as well as nailed to the back edges of the sides. This completes the basic box.

Cut two shelves, trimmed to pointed ends, to fit exactly the confines of the interior, supporting them with cleats on the back and on the short bar of the L-sides. Cut and attach the front trim directly to the edges of the sides, top and bottom, adding, at last, the 5 slim strips of horizontal trim and the crown or head piece. Since wall surfaces vary, no list of materials is included with this project.

PROJECT 65—
BEDSIDE STEP-TABLE

A forerunner of the standard night table in the modern bedroom, this colonial bedside table displays the typical qualities of early American furniture. It is simple and serviceable, yet reminiscent of the heritage of the pioneer families as tempered by the needs of frontier living and adapted by colonial craftsmen. Its design makes it a welcome complement to many popular furniture styles.

The table is constructed of ¾ inch pine. Cut the sides according to the pattern and bevel the tops at a 45 degree angle to form a miter joint with the top of the table. Notch the sides to receive the front and rear crosspieces. Cut and attach the crosspieces squarely to the ends with glue and finishing nails, then set the lower shelf in place between these pieces, gluing and nailing through both crosspieces and sides. Next, cut the top, bevel both ends and secure it in place, gluing and nailing the miter joint. Fasten the middle shelf with glue and finishing nails driven through the sides and rear crosspiece.

Assemble the drawer frame around the plywood bottom. Place triangular wood blocks in the front corners for reinforcement; these blocks are fastened to the sides and screwed into the front piece from inside. The drawer pulls are crafted from 1 inch hardwood dowels and sanded to shape and fastened by screws through predrilled holes in the drawer front.

LIST OF MATERIALS
A. One piece, 20″x11½″x¾″
B. Two pieces, each 25½″x16″x¾″
C. One piece, 20″x2¼″x¾″
D. One piece, 18½″x16″x¾″
E. One piece, 18½″x15¼″x¾″
F. One drawer: one front, 18½″x5½″x¾″; sides, 15″x5⅛″x⅜″; back, 17¾″x5⅛″x⅜″; bottom, 17¾″x14⅝″x⅜″
G. One piece, 20″x9½″x¾″

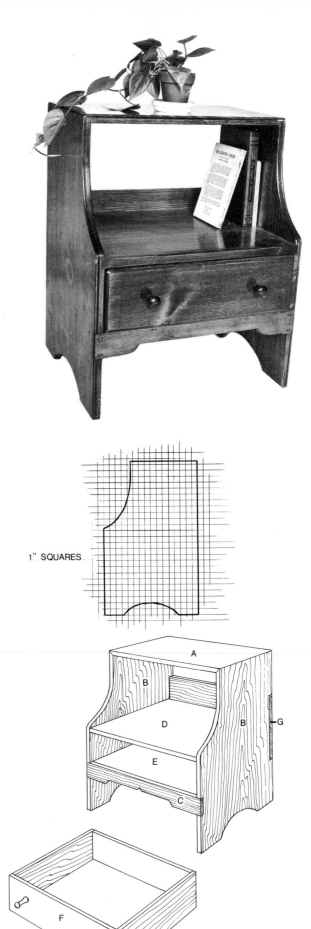

1″ SQUARES

EARLY AMERICAN FURNITURE
FINISHING

After completing the woodworking phase of early American furniture making, you are ready to add the finishing touches. A good finish on the furniture will add much to its appearance. No matter how good your workmanship or the quality of the lumber used, a poor finish will result in an unsatisfactory job. Therefore, decide upon the best finish for your particular purpose and apply it carefully.

PREPARATION OF WOOD

Authentic pieces of early Americana often bear the marks of the crude hand tools that were used in their making. Many of the finer reproductions sold so widely nowadays are painstakingly scarred and dented to simulate not only the handmade look but the evidence of age, as well. You can achieve this effect by first sanding all edges and surfaces velvety smooth.

All marks left on the wood after construction must be removed. Rough edges left by the saw should be sanded until perfectly smooth. If they are very rough, touch them up with the jointer before sanding. Dents in wood that you do not want can be eliminated by pricking the wood slightly with a sharp-pointed tool and then applying a few drops of water. The water will make the wood fibers swell back to the original shape. After the area is dry, sand the rough surface.

Joints that are not as tight as they should be can be filled with a wood filler. The seam should be cleaned and then packed with a filler such as plastic wood or spackle. As these fillers shrink slightly when dry, use a little more than required. An excellent homemade filler is wood glue mixed with sawdust; use the same sort of sawdust, when possible, as the wood to be filled. After the filler is dry, shave down the excess with a razor blade and then sand. Similarly, cracks in end grain and other spots should also be filled.

Nailheads should be punched below the wood surface and the resulting hole filled with wood filler. Screwheads that have been countersunk can be treated in the same manner. However, a more professional method is to glue a wood plug on top of the screwhead (see page 37).

Check all joints to be sure they are solid. If they do not appear to be strong enough, additional nails or screws may be necessary. In some cases, metal angle irons or wood blocks may be required.

When an assembly is completed and ready for finishing, go over the job carefully with at least three grades of sandpaper (see the table for abrasive data), using successively finer grits of garnet paper or cloth. If you do a good job when power sanding, you will only have to go over it lightly by hand with fine-grade paper.

WORD DESCRIPTION	GRIT	GRADE	USE
	600	——	
	500	——	
Superfine	400	10/0	
	360	9/0	Polishing and finishing
	320	——	
Extra fine	280	8/0	
	240	7/0	
Very fine	220	6/0	
Fine	180	5/0	
	150	4/0	Finishing
	120	3/0	Finishing
	100	2/0	
Medium	80	0 or 1/0	
	60	½	Cabinet
	50	1	
Coarse	40	1½	
	36	2	Rough Sanding
	30	2½	
Very Coarse	24	3	Coarse Sanding
	20	3½	

All sanding should be done in the direction of the wood grain. If the sanding is done by hand, make a sanding block with a felt pad attached to the underside. This does a better, faster job than if the sandpaper is pushed by hand alone.

If you wish to give the furniture a distressed appearance, use a rasp judiciously to make edge look irregular. Round all the corners, too. A few deep scratches here and there, made with a blunted nail, impart the appearance of age. Sand the treated areas to remove any burrs or splinters. After these preparatory steps have been taken, the wood is ready for finishing.

APPLYING THE FINISH

After the piece has been prepared and given a final sanding, you can apply the desired finish to your early American piece. Here are the basic steps in such a finishing operation:

1. Before you apply any finish, make certain surface is smooth, dry and dust-free.

2. Test finish on an unexposed surface of the piece or a scrap piece of the same lumber.

3. Brush or wipe on stain or finish quickly and evenly avoiding overlaps.

4. If a darker finish is desired, apply several coats one after the other.

5. Try to work on horizontal surfaces; otherwise wipe off runs and sags as soon as they appear.

6. Take it easy on end-grains; do not apply too much of the finish.

7. Do the inside and underparts first; final application is on top, sides and front.

8. Let dry in a dust-free room where the temperature remains above 70 degrees for at least 24 hours.

9. Do not smooth off until you have applied a sealer coat over any stain.

STAINS AND STAINING. Most projects in Section II require a stain to bring out the early American feeling of the furniture piece. There are many types of stains, but water stains and oil stains are the most common.

WATER STAINS. Water alcohol stains may be purchased in powder form in a variety of colors and mixed as needed by dissolving the powder in hot water. Water stain can be sprayed or brushed. Since the water in the stain raises the grain of the wood, a previous sponging with warm water is advisable.

Some workers prefer a small amount of dextrin in the sponging water to stiffen the wood fibers— 2 ounces per gallon. Dextrin, also known as starch gum, can be obtained at any wallpaper store.

When the wood is dry, sand it with fine paper. Then apply the stain freely and rapidly. Better penetration is obtained if the stain is used warm. Brush on the stain in long, smooth strokes, with the grain. Wiping the end grain with a cloth will prevent darkening. Other methods used to prevent darkening of end grain include (1) previous treatment with a thin glue size, (2) sponging with water immediately before staining, and (3) using a separate light stain.

Water stain will dry overnight or in 12 hours. A wash coat of 7 parts alcohol to 1 part shellac can be applied when the stain is dry. A light sanding will then remove any remaining traces of raised grain. Alcohol stains dry much faster.

Manufacturers have developed stains in which water-soluble powders are dissolved in a solvent other than water. Stains of this kind are known by various descriptive trade terms, such as non-grain-raising stain, fast-to-light stain, non-sand stain, etc. They are more expensive than regular water stains because of the solvent used, but offer some of the best stains for new work. Their rapid drying makes brushing difficult, but smooth coats are easily applied by spraying. They are non-bleeding and can be used under any type of finish coat. They dry in 10 minutes to 3 hours, depending on the type. Ready-mixed colors are numerous. Primary colors are available for mixing tints to suit individual tastes.

OIL STAINS. The most commonly used oil stains are made from colors or pigments ground in linseed oil. Oil is non-grain-raising; therefore oil stains do not require previous sponging. They

COLOR GUIDE FOR MIXING COLORS IN OIL
IF YOU MIX YOUR OWN

COLOR YOU WANT	USE BASE OF	ADD TO BASE VERY SMALL AMOUNT OF
Cherry (light)	Burnt sienna	Raw sienna
(dark)	Burnt sienna	Burnt umber
Maple (yellowish)	Raw sienna	Raw umber
(reddish)	Burnt sienna	Burnt umber
(blend)	Raw sienna	Burnt sienna + raw umber or burnt umber
Oak (light)	Raw sienna	Raw umber
Pine (warm brown)	Raw sienna	Ultramarine or deep Thalo green
(honey)	Yellow ocher	Raw sienna
Walnut (dark brown)	Burnt umber	Vandyke brown
(reddish-brown)	Burnt umber	Burnt sienna
(yellowish brown)	Burnt umber	Raw umber

Mix together: 3 parts commercially boiled linseed oil
1 part gum turpentine
½ part japan drier

can be brushed or sprayed on. The main difference in technique between water and oil staining is that oil stain is dipped with a rag to remove the surplus and equalize the color. Wiping is done while the stain is wet, but time should be allowed to ensure good penetration. Immediate wiping of the end grain will eliminate darkening. Since oil stains will bleed into finishing coats of varnish and lacquer, always seal the stain with a wash coat of shellac.

If you wish to mix your own oil stain colors using tubes of colors in oil, the basic colors are:
Red—burnt sienna.
Yellows—raw sienna, yellow ocher.
Browns—burnt umber, Vandyke brown, raw umber.
Greens (to dull reds)—deep Thalo green, medium green chrome.
Blacks—lampblack, ivory black.
Combine the colors-in-oil according to the color guide above. Soften the pigments in turpentine and add slowly in small amounts to the mixture described below in the chart, mixing thoroughly, until the desired color is attained.

FILLERS AND SEALERS. A filler is used to fill the pores in coarse-grain woods before applying the final finish. A sealer is any liquid finishing material used as a first coat on close-grain wood or over the filler on coarse-grain woods.

Prepared paste filler is generally the best for

FILLER FOR VARIOUS EARLY AMERICAN FURNITURE WOODS

NO FILLER NEEDED	LIQUID OR THIN PASTE	PASTE FILLER
Cedar	Birch	Ash
Fir	Cherry	Chestnut
Hemlock	Gum	Elm
Pine	Maple	Hickory
Poplar		Oak
Spruce		Walnut

home craftsmen. It may be purchased in a number of colors; select a shade slightly darker than the color of your wood, for the wood will gradually turn darker as it ages. If the desired color cannot be obtained, get a light color and add colored pigment in oil.

Liquid filler is generally a cheap varnish with a small amount of silex added. It is used on cheap work in medium close-grain woods. For a better grade of work a thin paste filler is more satisfactory. The table lists the various woods and the type of filler, if any, required for each.

Before using paste filler, thin it with a small amount of turpentine or naphtha until it is of the proper consistency to brush. Wood with coarse pores will require a thicker filler than wood with small pores.

To apply the filler, use a fairly stiff brush. Brushing is done with the grain, in order to pack the filler into the pores. In 5 to 20 minutes, the filler will start to lose its wet appearance. As soon as spots begin to flat out, take a piece of burlap and pad the filler into the pores. Clean off the surplus by wiping across the grain; and finish wiping with clean rags, stroking with the grain. If the filler sets up too hard for easy wiping, moisten the wiping rag with benzine.

Inspect the entire project thoroughly. If the pores are not filled level, apply a second coat of slightly thinner filler immediately, wiping off in the same way. Paste filler should dry for 12 to 24 hours, unless it is a fast-drying type, which is ready in 3 to 4 hours. In any case, it is of the greatest importance that the filler be bone dry before any other coating is applied. The dry filler should be sanded lightly with fine or very fine garnet or aluminum oxide paper and wiped off with a rag moistened with benzine.

Whether or not to seal the filler is largely a matter of preference. The same applies to sealing the stain coat before applying the filler, except in the case of softwoods, such as fir, which must be sealed before staining. Generally, it is good practice to seal both stain and filler. A special resin sealer is best for the job, but for many people shellac is the old standby—white shellac for light finishes and orange shellac for browns and mahoganies. The shellac is reduced with alcohol (4 to 1 for filler sealer, 7 to 1 for stain sealer), after which the shellac is poured slowly into an equal amount or less of mixing lacquer. This mixture can be brushed on more easily than straight shellac, is almost waterproof, and dries to permit recoating in about 2 hours. Any type of sealer coat over the filler should be sanded with fine paper when dry, after which the work is ready for finishing coats of varnish or lacquer.

VARNISH FINISHES. Varnish makes an excellent transparent finish on wood, being unequaled for depth or build and possessing good durability and hardness. It brushes easily to a perfectly smooth film and dries to permit recoating in 12 to 48 hours. Varnishing should be done in a dust-free room, between 70 and 80 degrees Fahrenheit. Some craftsmen sprinkle the floor with water to settle the dust. Before applying the varnish, dampen a piece of lintless cloth in a little varnish and wipe the surface with it. The small amount of varnish in the cloth will pick up dust which would not otherwise be caught.

Be sure to follow the manufacturer's instructions on the container. As a rule, spread the varnish on as it comes from the can—evenly with long strokes, first with the grain, then across the grain, and then with the grain. As varnish is slow-drying, thinned shellac is often used for a sealer coat. The shellac dries quickly and does not soak into the wood, thus speeding up the drying of the varnish.

A good varnished surface usually requires two or three coats. Rub each coat down with fine steel wool or extra-fine sandpaper, after letting the varnish dry for at least 48 hours. Remove all dust from the surface, after sanding, by rubbing with a lint-free cloth moistened with turpentine or a chamois dampened with water. Pumice and oil, followed with rottenstone and oil, will produce a finely polished surface.

SHELLAC FINISHES. Shellac makes a good finish for many pieces of furniture. It is hard, quite easy to apply, dries in a few hours, and does not require a dustproofer.

Since shellac dries very quickly, you must work fast with it, or it will become tacky and hard to handle. Never apply shellac over a damp surface, for the moisture will cause the shellac to become cloudy. Brush with the grain of the wood and do not brush too much. For best results, dilute the shellac with alcohol. It is easier to apply thinned shellac, and (unless you are experienced in applying it unthinned) you will generally get a better-finished surface. Several coats of thin shellac are best for a well-finished surface.

Standard shellac ordinarily dries hard in about 8 hours, although thinned shellac dries in 3 or 4 hours, ready for sanding. Go over each coat with fine sandpaper or 2/0 fine steel wool. Sandpaper with the grain of the wood. After each sanding, brush the surface and rub with a cloth dampened with benzine to remove the dust. The final rubbing or polishing should be done with FF pumice stone and rubbing oil, using a felt pad.

LACQUER FINISHES. Roughly speaking, lacquer can be divided into two groups—brushing lacquer and spraying lacquer. Lacquers dry very rapidly. Generally, spraying lacquers dry so rapidly that they cannot be applied with a brush.

The solvent used with the lacquer for thinning or as a cleaner for brushes or a spray gun is lacquer thinner. Thinners suitable for paint and varnish should never be used with lacquer. While paint and varnish can be applied over lacquer, lacquer should never be applied over paint or varnish because the solvent in the lacquer will soften these base coats.

Brushing Lacquer. To apply brushing lacquer properly, you must work with a good deal of speed. The lacquer should be flowed on and brushed out as little as possible. Use a large brush and let it carry as much lacquer as possible without dripping. Apply the lacquer in one direction only. If a second coat is required, it must be applied with even more speed, or the solvent in the second coat will soften the first coat.

Spraying Lacquer. By far the best method of applying lacquer is to use a spray gun, but this calls for good equipment.

RUBBING WITH PUMICE AND ROTTEN-STONE. A fine finish for varnish, lacquer, and shellac is obtained by rubbing with pumice or rottenstone. Mix the pumice with either water or oil (paraffin or mineral), and use a felt pad to rub the paste over the finished surface. Rub with the grain. Use pumice with oil, not with water, on shellac finish. Rub until the desired finish is obtained. Rottenstone is much finer than pumice and is used in the same manner, usually following a rubbing with pumice.

If water is used with either pumice or rottenstone, it makes the mixture cut faster and produces a duller finish. When rubbing edges, corners, and high spots, be very careful not to cut through the finish. Clean the surface thoroughly with a soft rag after rubbing.

WAX FINISHES. A wax finish has a pleasing eggshell gloss and is satisfactory for furniture as well as for floors and woodwork. Fill the wood and give a sealing coat of thinned shellac, lacquer, or varnish, and allow to dry. Sandpaper lightly before applying the wax.

Rub the wax on the surface, a little at a time, with a soft cloth. Allow to dry for about 20 minutes, and then rub hard with a soft cloth. Several coats are usually required.

PENETRATING RESIN-OIL FINISHES. These are a fairly new type of finish put out by many homecraft furniture makers. They actually improve the wood permanently without hours of hand rubbing, yet give that lustrous hand-rubbed look with a simple application that is longer lasting, seldom needs replenishing, never needs resanding.

While you should always follow the manufacturer's specific instructions, here are the basic ones for applying penetrating resin-oil finishes:

After the stain has dried, liberally apply the penetrating resin-oil finish. Allow to soak in until penetration stops (about 30 minutes), keeping the wood surface uniformly wet at all times. Now, and most important, wipe the surface completely dry. None of the penetrating resin-oil finish should be left standing to dry on the wood surface.

You will then have a handsome satin finish. While it is not meant to compete with the glossy surface finishes which were popular a few years ago, more luster is possible. Simply wait about four hours—preferably, overnight—after drying the surface of excess resin-oil, then, using a small amount of resin-oil finish or camauba (palm oil) satin wax as a lubricant, wet sand lightly, wait about ten minutes and wipe clean and dry. Polish with a soft cloth.

Most penetrating resin-oil finishes may be applied easily in almost any climate under normal atmospheric conditions (dirt-free air not required). Apply by spraying, dipping, brushing or any conventional method. Penetrating resin-oil finishes should not be thinned or pre-heated. They are applied just as they come from the container.

OIL POLISH FINISH. To get a beautiful rich finish on hardwoods:

1. Brush boiled linseed oil on raw smoothly sanded furniture and let it soak in, then polish long and vigorously with a soft cloth.

2. Repeat each week until you have reached the desired color and sheen. Let dry for a few days.

3. Apply a thin coat of shellac and two coats of wax.

FINISHING SCHEDULES

Here are several basic finishing schedules that may be used when finishing the projects described in Section II.

HONEY COLOR MAPLE

1. Stain with weak walnut alcohol or water stain.
2. Dry 1½ hours.
3. Scuff with medium sandpaper.
4. Flow on thinned shellac with brush.
5. Dry four hours.
6. Cover with another coat of thinned shellac.
7. Dry overnight.
8. Rub with medium waterproof sandpaper. Lubricate with 8 parts Savasol #5 and 1 light rubbing oil or thin mineral spirits.
9. Rub with sandpaper, lubricate again as in step 8.
10. Wax with good paste wax, let dry 20 minutes and buff.

KNOTTY PINE FINISH

1. Sand surfaces smooth to touch with fine sandpaper. Dust.
2. Apply very light pine or oak water or alcohol stain to depth of color desired and according to manufacturer's directions. Dry overnight. Flow on thinned shellac. Do not go over wet shellacked areas. Allow the first coat to dry three hours.
3. Steel-wool lightly with #3/0 and dust.
4. Apply second coat thinned shellac and dry overnight.
5. Rub with fine Wet-or-Dry sandpaper and machine oil, with the grain. For a smooth luster, wax, let dry for 20 minutes and buff.

ANTIQUE PINE FINISH. This is well-suited for finishing colonial antique reproductions. The antique pine stain, slightly redder than ordinary pine stains, is made by several manufacturers.

1. After the piece is thoroughly sanded and cleaned, apply stain with brush or cloth, following technique previously mentioned.
2. Wipe off excess and apply another coat if darker tone is wanted.
3. Sand lightly with 3/0 sandpaper and apply a protective coat of wax, 50-50 shellac-and-alcohol or varnish. Then polish briskly with soft cloth or lamb's wool.

BLEACHING. Bleaching lightens the color of

wood by means of chemicals. Apart from the bleaching process, the so-called blond finishes do not differ in any way from other finishes. Not all blond finishes are secured by bleaching. Maple, birch, and other light-colored woods are successfully blonded by the use of a pigmented undercoat. This subject is treated at the end of this section.

Simple homemade bleaches are 100 per cent effective on light-colored woods and will lighten any dark wood to a considerable extent. Typical of these is the simple oxalic acid bleach, which is inexpensive and easy to make. Three solutions are required: (1) 3 ounces of oxalic acid crystals dissolved in 1 quart of water, (2) 3 ounces of sodium hyposulfite (photo hypo) in 1 quart of water, and (3) 1 ounce of borax in 1 quart of water. These chemicals can be obtained from any drugstore at a small cost.

All solutions are made with hot water but are used cold. The oxalic acid solution is applied first, with a brush or rubber sponge. When this coat has partly dried, the second solution (hypo) is applied, after which the work should be allowed to dry thoroughly. If the color of the wood is not light enough, the process can be repeated. When the color is right, the surface should be flushed with the borax solution. Overnight drying should be allowed before sanding. The work is then ready for any kind of varnish or lacquer finish.

There are several prepared commercial bleaches which are high-powered enough to give nearly white tones on walnut and mahogany in a single application. The procedure for applying these bleaches varies with the brand, and the manufacturer's directions must be followed. After the work is completely dry, it should be sanded lightly with very fine sandpaper to remove any chemical residue and to clean up wood fibers lifted by the bleaching solution.

Wood is usually bleached a bit more than is required for the final finish. The color is brought back to the desired shade with a light application of non-grain-raising stain, applied in such a manner as to equalize any variations in color. The stain is followed by a wash coat of shellac or lacquer, after which the regular schedule of filler and top coat completes the finish.

BLOND SEALERS. Excellent blond finishes can be obtained without bleaching by using a surface color or blond sealer. This is a very satisfactory method of treating naturally light woods. Add white lacquer enamel to clear lacquer, or, if an amber effect is desired, add tan to clear lacquer. Blond sealers of this kind can be purchased ready mixed. A uniform, light coat of the sealer will produce a satisfactory blond color without obscuring the natural grain of the wood. This blonding technique is perfect on maple and birch and can be used on walnut to produce a pleasing tone, a little lighter than the natural color of the wood. When overdone on dark-colored woods, it gives the wood a painted appearance and the effect is not pleasing. While it is true that blond or bleached finishes are not "true" early American finishes, they are sometimes employed to blend with other furniture pieces in the room setting.

ENAMEL FINISH. While none of the furniture pieces illustrated in this book are enameled, some of them would be well suited for such a finish. To enamel early American furniture surfaces:

1. Follow the steps outlined for cleaning and preparing the surface described earlier in the text.

2. Seal the wood with a wash coat of shellac (50 per cent shellac-50 per cent denatured alcohol). The shellac will help prevent the grain from showing through the enamel.

3. After the shellac is dry, smooth lightly with #3/0 steel wool. Sandpaper does not work too well because shellac has a tendency to clog.

4. Tint the enamel undercoat if you plan a single finishing coat of dark enamel. Mix ¾ of the undercoat with ¼ of the enamel to be used. Enamel undercoat needs a thorough stirring. Pour off the top liquid, stir the pigment until it

is smooth, return the liquid slowly as you stir it in.

5. Apply the undercoat and brush it out thoroughly. Avoid a heavy, gummy undercoat. Do not overload your brush. Start painting at a top piece on the furniture and work down. Watch carefully for sags and runs, brush them out before they harden.

6. Smooth the undercoat with #4/0 to #6/0 sandpaper after you have permitted the surface to dry for at least 24 hours. Use a light touch on the undercoat because it is a soft surface and easy to cut through into the wood. Dust with a turpentine-soaked rag.

7. If two or more colors are to be used, apply masking tape to stop the finishing coats on a straight line and to prevent running. Brush on the finish and strip off the tape *before* the finish hardens. Flow on enamel in small squares and smooth with a very light cross brushing. Dip in only half of the brush to avoid overloading with enamel. Work rapidly and don't overbrush.

8. One coat usually will cover; two will add durability. Roughen the first coat slightly with fine sandpaper after it dries and before you apply the second coat. A good wax can be applied if desired, for added protection.

ANTIQUED FINISH. Antiquing over enamel is a glaze or toner coat that is used to obtain a mellow or soft appearance rather than a finish that will simulate great age. The finish is achieved by a glaze coat colored with oil colors applied over a base-coat enamel in a lighter value. When the glaze coat is sparingly and carefully applied, the result should give a pleasing effect. Actually, a glazed finish is more effective when applied to furniture with carved surfaces, moldings, and turnings rather than to a piece that is entirely flat in design.

The furniture piece to be enameled is prepared in the same manner as a piece that will not have a glazed finish, with the exception of the final rub of pumice and oil. Make a "tooth" for the glazing liquid on the final coat of enamel by

lightly rubbing with 3/0 steel wool or a fine-grit abrasive paper. Wipe the sandings from the piece with a clean cloth or tack rag. The piece is now ready for the glaze application.

You may prepare your own glazing liquid or purchase one that is ready mixed. Prepare a glazing liquid by mixing 3 tablespoons gum turpentine, 1 tablespoon varnish or boiled linseed oil (varnish preferred), and 1 teaspoon of the desired oil color(s). Stir well until uniformly mixed.

Examples of glaze oil colors to use over ivory or off-white base enamels to achieve a mellow look are:

Raw umber (grayish tone)
Raw sienna (reddish tone)
Burnt umber (brownish tone)
Burnt sienna (reddish-brown tone)

Other hues are equally effective, depending upon the enamel color and the color scheme of the room in which the finished piece will be used. Ready mixed glazing liquid can be purchased from a paint or art store in a variety of colors. Follow application directions.

APPLYING THE GLAZE. Wipe the enameled undercoat surface with a tack rag to remove all traces of dust and dirt. Then mix the glazing liquid and oil colors thoroughly. If using a commercial glazing liquid, stir it thoroughly with a wooden paddle and read the label instructions carefully.

Apply a thin coat of the glazing liquid with an oil paint brush, painting one side of the piece of furniture at a time. Long, even strokes with the grain of the wood will produce the best results. If the piece has prominent legs, turn it upside down and paint the legs first, then the top, working downward. Pay special attention to carved trim and crevices, painting them first to allow more absorption of the glaze.

Let the color glaze set for 10 to 30 minutes before beginning to rub or wipe.

WIPING THE GLAZE. Once the glaze has set

enough to be slightly "tacky" use cheesecloth to wipe lightly at first and then more heavily in those places where you want more highlights— usually the high points of carving and the center of panels. Wipe in long, straight lines in the direction of the grain (usually the long way to your piece).

Blend further by patting the surface with clean cheesecloth and finish blending with a dry paint brush. Work the brush from the center toward the edges. Wipe the brush off on a cloth to remove excess glaze. Wiping off and blending is not at all difficult when only a small amount of glaze material remains on the surface. It gives a slightly noticeable but most effective appearance.

Rub large, flat areas in long, even strokes, beginning with a light touch and applying more pressure as you get along. If you find that you have allowed the glaze to set too long, simply dampen your rubbing cloth with mineral spirits. If wiping shows that you haven't allowed the glaze to set long enough, simply apply another coat and wait again.

For carved surfaces, moldings, and turnings, proceed as for flat surfaces. Remove excess glaze material from depressions with a dry paint brush. Wipe the brush off on a cloth. Highlight by wiping the glaze off the raised areas with a clean cloth, leaving the glaze in the depressions for contrast. Difficulty in rubbing intricate carved trim can be overcome by using a cotton tip in those hard-to-reach areas.

When you have finished wiping, allow enough time for the paint to dry thoroughly, usually 24 hours. In some commercial antiquing systems a second coat of glaze is required. This second coat is applied in the same manner as the first.

A glazing liquid you have prepared yourself should have a protective coat for greater wear and durability. When the glaze is completely dry, apply a coat of *water-clear varnish*. (Do not use regular varnish as it has a yellowish color.) Allow one week for the varnish to dry. If the surface is too shiny, rub carefully with 4/F or 3/F pumice

powder and mineral oil. Make a paste of the powder and mineral oil and apply with your hands. Rub the surface until a satin finish is obtained. Wipe the surface with a clean, dry cloth to remove the pumice and oil.

A commercial glazing liquid may also require a protective coat. The label will state if a protective coat is needed. If it is, then purchase the protective coat in the same brand as the glazing liquid.

With either commercial or homemade glazing liquid, if you wish to wax the surface, it is best to allow the paint to dry for at least a week before applying.

FINISHING FIR PLYWOOD. Fir plywood needs a good sealer, because of the special character of the grain which is made up of alternate hard summer growth and softer spring growth. Without a sealer, the first coat of paint or stain penetrates unevenly, resulting usually in a "wild," overly conspicuous grain. To "tame" or quiet this grain, several special types of sealers are available; they allow the stain to soften the darker markings and deepen the lighter surfaces.

To obtain a light natural finish, sandpaper the wood with medium sandpaper, and then apply an even coat of resin sealer. Lightly sand when dry, and follow with a thin coat of pure white shellac; the shellac should be reduced to 2-pound cut. Sandpaper again when dry and apply either a satin-finish lacquer or a gloss varnish. If a flat finish is desired, a flat or dull varnish may be substituted. After it is thoroughly dry, steel-wool the surface and apply white wax.

FINISHING HARDBOARD. Practically any type of finishing material may be used on hardboard —oil paint, water paint, enamel, stain, lacquer, shellac, varnish, penetrating sealers, wax, and special finishes. By following the manufacturer's directions and applying the finishes in the same manner as on a hardwood surface, satisfactory results are obtained. The surface must be free of all dirt, grease, and other foreign material before a finish is applied. Dirt may be removed with water and a mild soap, and grease with naphtha.

Be sure the hardboard panel is dry before starting to finish it.

HOW TO FINISH A RUSH SEAT

After you have completed the weaving and padding, trim the butt ends on the lower side of the seat to about 1 inch, so that they do not show as you face the chair. Trim any loose ends with a razor blade or shears. Use the rounded end of the stuffer to pound and even the seat. On the upper side, trim the loose ends, straighten the rows, and pound with the stuffer to mold and polish the twists. You may also use a piece of leather for polishing.

Immediately after you finish weaving, apply a protective coating both to the top and to the lower side of the seat. One treatment is as follows: Apply a mixture of half turpentine and half raw linseed oil (4 tablespoons each) to both sides of the seat. The next day, when this is dry, apply a second coat (about 3 tablespoons of each), and when this is thoroughly dry, apply a coat of dull varnish. Add coats of varnish until there are no dull spots on the rush.

When first and second coats are still "tacky," smooth and even the strands so that when the varnish sets they will be held in place. Shellac may be used instead of the above mixture.

Be sure no one sits in the chair until the finish has dried thoroughly, at least two weeks after the weaving is completed.

HOW TO FINISH A SPLINT SEAT

Trim off hairs or rough places with a razor blade or sharp knife. Splint that has a hard, glossy surface can be left without a finish. Or you may apply two or three coats of a thin type of penetrating wood sealer to both sides of the seat. Apply the first coat as soon as you finish weaving. Let each coat dry thoroughly before applying the next. If you want the seat darkened to blend with the color of the chair finish, apply one or more coats of seat stain, which you can obtain from the dealer from whom you buy other seating supplies. A sealer can then be used over the stain. Wax can also be used, but it may stain clothing and collect dust.

Index